Year-Round Crafts for KIDS

pil

Publications International, Ltd.

Contributing Designers: Lori Blankenship, Lisa Galvin, Heidi King, and Sherri Osborn
Contributing Illustrators: Barbara Ball and Connie Formby
Icon Illustrators: Terri and Joe Chicko

Louis Weber, CEO
Publications International, Ltd.
7373 North Cicero Avenue
Lincolnwood, Illinois 60712

Permission is never granted for commercial purposes.

Manufactured in China.

8 7 6 5 4 3 2 1

ISBN: 0-7853-8840-0

Library of Congress Control Number: 2003104001

Contents

Year-Round Crafts Mean Year-Round Fun!

Dear Parents,

Just about everyone has made a Thanksgiving turkey out of their handprint or homemade Valentines for their family and friends. But there are so many other crafty ways to celebrate the holidays!

Year-Round Crafts for Kids offers tons of fun, interesting projects that will keep your children busy the whole year long. From springtime flower bouquets and back-to-school projects to super summer flip-flops and way cool Christmas ornaments, kids can find crafts for all of their favorite holidays plus projects to commemorate the changing seasons. Best of all, some of the projects offer information about different cultures of the world and many may provide children with skills that could help them in school and everyday life.

Divided into four sections—Spring, Summer, Fall, and Winter—the book includes simple crafts that require common craft materials, many of which you can probably find in your own home. Each project includes a list of materials needed to complete the craft as well as easy-to-follow instructions and step-by-step illustrations. Take the time to go over the instructions carefully, and make sure you have all the materials on hand before you get started. Here are just a few of the materials that are required for most projects:

- Paper: Since many of the book's projects include patterns or stencils that will need to be traced and cut out, be sure to have plenty of tracing paper. When a project calls for scrap paper, recycle some of that computer paper and junk mail you have lying around the house!

- Glue: Most projects call for craft, or white, glue. This is a waterbase glue that can be thinned for easy application. Fabric glue, which is not water-soluble, holds up better outdoors or in projects that will be washed. You'll also need a glue gun for some of the projects. Be sure to set the glue gun on low, and keep an eye on your child while he or she is using it.

- Paint: Waterbase acrylic paint is listed most frequently for the projects in this book. It is a vibrant form of paint that can be used on all surfaces. Acrylic paint dries permanently, but when wet it is easily cleaned up with water. Make sure your children clean painting tools thoroughly when they are finished painting.

- Chenille stems: Most chenille stems come in 12-inch lengths, so when a project calls for a chenille stem, that means a 12-inch stem.

- Art smock: Make sure your child wears a smock or one of your old shirts to protect clothes while working with paints and other messy materials such as clay.

Some children will be able to complete the crafts with little help, but there will be times when your assistance is needed. Other projects just need a watchful eye. So it's best if you and your child review the project together and then make a decision about your role.

Completing the projects in *Year-Round Crafts for Kids* should be an enjoyable, creative, energizing experience for your child. Encourage kids to create their own versions of projects, using their imagination as their guide. And don't forget to admire and praise the wonderful results!

Hey, Kids!

The changing seasons can bring about so many fun things— the first day of school, the *last* day of school, the first snowfall, the first picnic at the park. Well, now you can celebrate these and so many other events and holidays with cool craft projects!

Year-Round Crafts for Kids is filled with ideas for arts and crafts projects, many of which make great gifts for family and friends. Although we know you'll want to get started on the projects right away, please read these few basic steps before beginning.

- For any project or activity you decide to do, gather all your materials, remembering to ask permission first. If you need to purchase materials, take along this book, or make a shopping list so you know exactly what you need.
- Prepare your work area ahead of time, including covering any surface you work on with newspapers or an old, plastic tablecloth. Ask an adult if you're not sure whether to cover the kitchen table—but remember, it's better to be safe than sorry!
- Wear an apron or a smock when painting with acrylic paints; after the paint dries, it is permanent. If you do get paint on your clothes, wash them with soap and warm water immediately.
- Be sure an adult is nearby to offer help if you need it. And adult help is always needed if you will be using a glue gun, a craft knife, an oven, or anything else that may be dangerous.
- Be careful not to put any materials near your mouth. And make sure to watch out for small items, such as beads, around little kids and pets.
- When using a glue gun, be sure to put it on the low-temperature setting. Do not touch the nozzle or the freshly applied glue; it may still be hot. And use the glue gun with adult permission only!

- Clean up afterward, and put away all materials and tools. Leaving a mess one time may mean you hear the word "no" the next time you ask to make something!
- Have fun, and be creative!

Pattern Perfect

Many of the projects featured in this book include patterns to help you complete the craft more easily. When a project's instructions tell you to cut out a shape according to the pattern, trace the pattern from the book onto tracing paper, using a pencil. If the pattern has an arrow with the word *FOLD* next to a line, it is a half pattern. Fold a sheet of tracing paper in half, and open up the paper. Place the fold line of the tracing paper exactly on top of the fold line of the pattern, and trace the pattern with a pencil. Then refold and cut along the line, going through both layers. Open the paper for the full pattern.

Turn to the back of the book to find several seasonal stencils, including flower shapes, a shamrock, autumn leaves, and a Christmas tree. These stencils will come in handy for a few of the projects in the book. You can even keep the stencils to use later for all kinds of projects!

Fold

Ready, Set, Go!

All of the projects presented in this book, from the simplest bookmark to the most elaborate beaded key chain, are just ideas to get you started crafting. Feel free to play around with the designs by changing the colors, choosing different materials, or embellishing in any number of unique ways. Once you are comfortable with these crafts, let your imagination really go wild and dream up some original crafts using these merely as a jumping-off point. There's no limit to what you can create!

What You'll Need

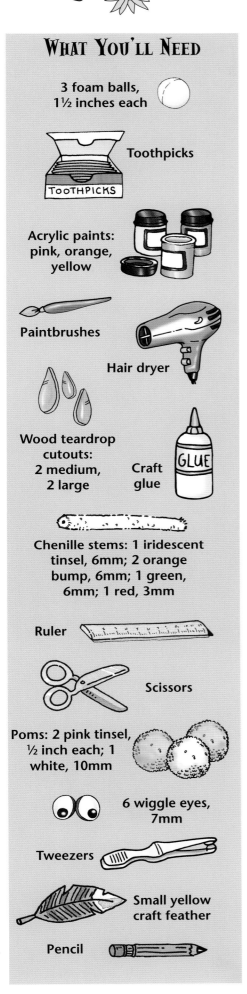

3 foam balls, 1½ inches each

Toothpicks

Acrylic paints: pink, orange, yellow

Paintbrushes

Hair dryer

Wood teardrop cutouts: 2 medium, 2 large

Craft glue

Chenille stems: 1 iridescent tinsel, 6mm; 2 orange bump, 6mm; 1 green, 6mm; 1 red, 3mm

Ruler

Scissors

Poms: 2 pink tinsel, ½ inch each; 1 white, 10mm

6 wiggle eyes, 7mm

Tweezers

Small yellow craft feather

Pencil

1 Insert a toothpick into each foam ball to help you handle the balls while you decorate them. Paint each ball a different color. Dry the balls with a hair dryer set on a warm temperature, turning them around to dry all sides. Paint 2 medium teardrops orange for the duckbill and 2 large teardrops pink for the bunny ears. Dry the cutouts with the hair dryer.

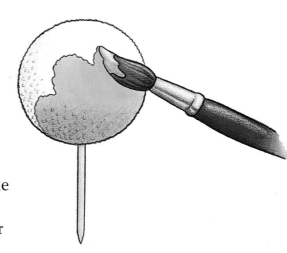

2 To make the bunny ears, put a drop of glue onto the pointed end of a pink teardrop shape and push the end into the top of the pink ball. Repeat for the other ear. Cut two 2½-inch lengths from the iridescent tinsel chenille stem. Fold one length in half and insert it into the ball just in front of an ear. Repeat with the other chenille stem piece for the other ear. For the bunny's cheeks, glue the pink tinsel poms side by side toward the bottom of the pink foam ball. Glue the white pom just above the cheeks for the nose. Use tweezers to help you glue on 2 wiggle eyes.

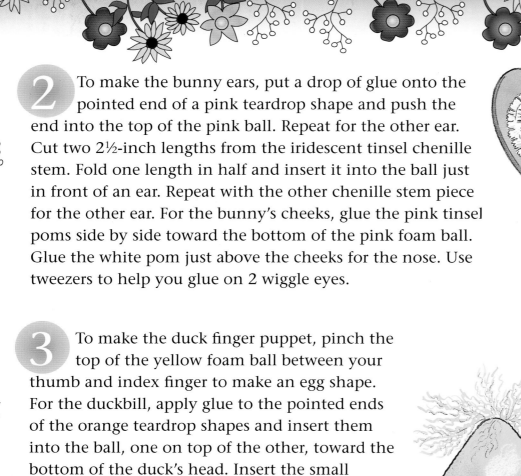

3 To make the duck finger puppet, pinch the top of the yellow foam ball between your thumb and index finger to make an egg shape. For the duckbill, apply glue to the pointed ends of the orange teardrop shapes and insert them into the ball, one on top of the other, toward the bottom of the duck's head. Insert the small yellow feather into the top of the head, and glue on 2 wiggle eyes.

4 For the flower finger puppet, cut the orange chenille stems apart between bumps. Bend each bump into a flower petal. Add a drop of glue to the ends of 1 petal and insert it into the side of the orange foam ball. Repeat with the remaining petals, working around the foam ball. Cut the green chenille stem in half, then fold each length to create 2 leaves. Put glue on the ends of the leaves and insert them into the ball behind the petals. Glue on 2 wiggle eyes. Cut 2 inches from the red chenille stem, and bend the piece into a smile. Attach the smile to the flower face with glue.

5 Use the sharpened end of the pencil to create a finger hole at the bottom of each finger puppet, gradually turning the pencil to make the hole large enough for your finger to fit into.

8 🌸 **Spring**

Petal Posies

What You'll Need

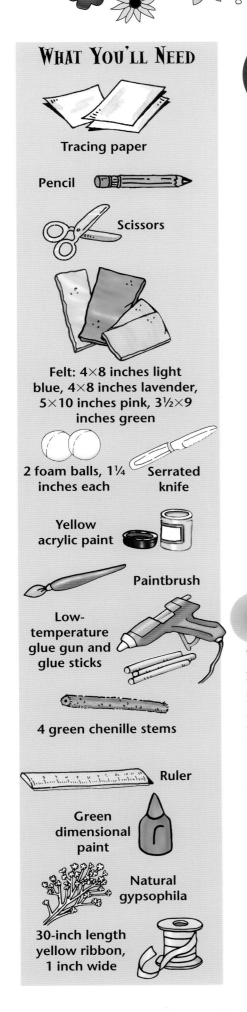

Tracing paper

Pencil

Scissors

Felt: 4×8 inches light blue, 4×8 inches lavender, 5×10 inches pink, 3½×9 inches green

2 foam balls, 1¼ inches each

Serrated knife

Yellow acrylic paint

Paintbrush

Low-temperature glue gun and glue sticks

4 green chenille stems

Ruler

Green dimensional paint

Natural gypsophila

30-inch length yellow ribbon, 1 inch wide

1. Use the patterns on page 11 to trace and cut out the following: 2 round flowers from light blue felt, 2 round flowers from lavender felt, 2 pointed flowers from pink felt, and 6 leaves from green felt. Have an adult help you cut the foam balls in half with the serrated knife. Paint 3 foam ball halves with yellow paint; discard the remaining ball half. Let paint dry, then apply another coat. Glue the flat side of a ball half to the center of 1 blue flower. To give the flower a dimensional look, apply a line of glue around the very bottom edge of the foam ball and bend up the petals around the ball. Hold until set (be careful, glue can be hot!). Repeat for 1 pink flower and 1 lavender flower; set aside the other flowers.

2 To make a flower stem, glue 1 inch of one end of a green chenille stem to the back of the blue felt flower. Align the edges of the flower with the other blue felt flower piece, sandwiching the chenille stem between them. Apply a line of glue between the layers near the edge, then press the edges together. Repeat for the pink and lavender flowers.

3 Add veins on the leaves with green dimensional paint; let dry. Glue 5 leaves to 3 flower stems; set aside the remaining leaf.

4 Add sprigs of gypsophila among the flowers. Make a bow out of the matching ribbon. Wrap the remaining chenille stem around the middle of the bow, then wrap the chenille stem around all the flower stems. Twist the chenille stem ends together in the back, then trim and fold over the ends. Glue the remaining leaf to the back of the uppermost flower.

Patterns

Stained Glass Easter Basket

What You'll Need

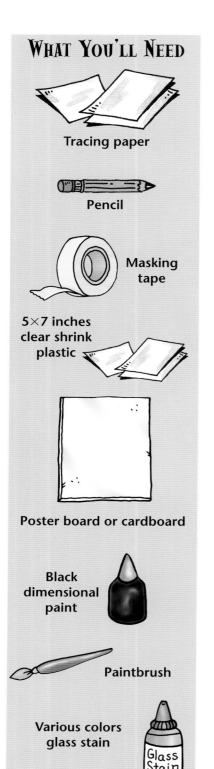

Tracing paper

Pencil

Masking tape

5×7 inches clear shrink plastic

Poster board or cardboard

Black dimensional paint

Paintbrush

Various colors glass stain

Pattern

1 Copy the pattern on page 12 onto tracing paper. Roll 4 pieces of masking tape into loops with the sticky side out; place them on the 4 corners of the tracing paper without covering any of the pattern. Set the piece of shrink plastic on the pattern with the edges properly aligned, and press down firmly until the tape holds the plastic in place. Place the shrink plastic and pattern on the poster board to protect your work surface.

2 Beginning with the horizontal line at the top of the pattern and working your way down, carefully trace the pattern onto the shrink plastic with the dimensional paint. It is important that all the lines and corners are solid so the different areas of the pattern are separated. If the paint smears, use a damp paintbrush to wipe away the smear. Let dry.

3 Remove the pattern from the shrink plastic, and set the plastic back on the poster board. Figure out what color scheme you would like to use before you begin to stain the shrink plastic. To prepare the stain, gently tip the bottles back and forth without shaking them (this prevents bubbles from forming). Apply 1 color of stain to 1 area of the shrink plastic, using the bottle nozzle to move the stain into the corners. Press any bubbles against the edge of a black paint line. Apply enough stain so it's bright in color but not so much that it runs over the dimensional paint lines. Repeat with the other colors to fill in the other areas. Let dry. Apply to a window, and let the sun shine through your basket of colorful Easter eggs!

Lucky Sprouts

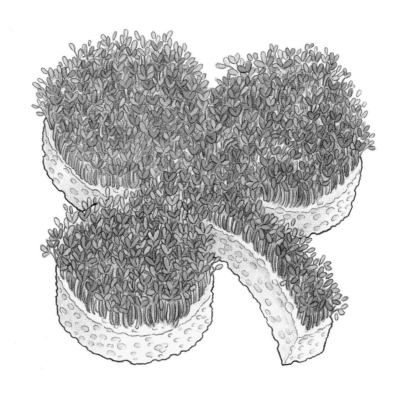

1 Use the shamrock stencil at the back of the book to help you trace and cut out a shamrock shape from the compressed sponge. Dampen the sponge so it expands, and squeeze out any extra water. Set the sponge on the plate or pie pan, and sprinkle the seeds on top of the sponge.

2 Your seeds should sprout in a few days (see instructions on the seed package) if you take good care of them! During the night, cover the sponge lightly with plastic wrap to help it stay moist. During the day, place your sponge in a sunny spot, making sure the sponge stays wet (water around the sponge; don't put water directly on the seeds).

3 For variety, draw and cut out different shapes from the compressed sponge. You can even try sprinkling seeds over just certain areas of the sponge. For example, you could cut out a shape that looks like a person's head and sprinkle the seeds over the area where hair would grow. Then you could draw on a face with markers. Pretend he's a leprechaun for even more luck!

Did You Know?
The first St. Patrick's Day parade took place not in Ireland but in New York City on March 17, 1762.

May Day Colorful Lei

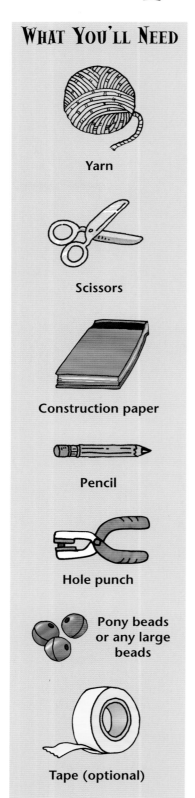

1 Cut a length of yarn to hang loosely around your neck (make sure you cut it a little longer than you want it so you have room to tie the ends of the yarn together). Using the flower stencils in the back of the book, trace and cut colorful flower shapes out of construction paper. (If you want flowers that will stand up to a little more wear and tear, make them out of craft foam; use tissue paper for more delicate flowers.) Punch a hole in the center of each flower.

2 To put your lei together, tie a knot at one end of the piece of yarn. String 6 to 10 beads onto the yarn (this will be the part of the lei that touches the back of your neck). Then alternate flowers and beads however you want. If you have a hard time stringing the beads onto the yarn, wrap a small piece of tape around the end of the yarn to stiffen it.

3 Once you get the design you want and the yarn is almost full of flowers and beads, end just as you started, with 6 to 10 beads. Tie the end in a knot. Then tie the two ends of the yarn together, and wear your lei with pride!

Did You Know?

May Day is celebrated as a festival marking the reappearance of flowers during the spring. People in Hawaii celebrate May Day by giving flower leis to each other.

Beautiful Button Quilt

Adult help needed

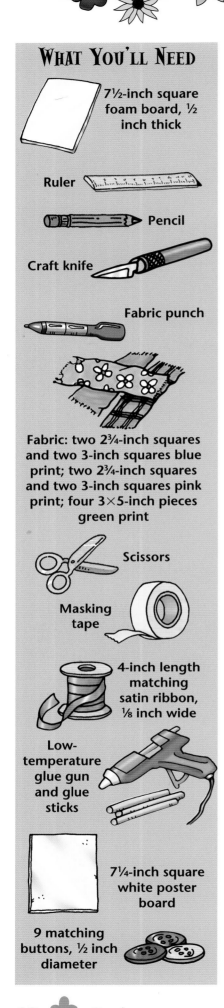

What You'll Need

- 7½-inch square foam board, ½ inch thick
- Ruler
- Pencil
- Craft knife
- Fabric punch
- Fabric: two 2¾-inch squares and two 3-inch squares blue print; two 2¾-inch squares and two 3-inch squares pink print; four 3×5-inch pieces green print
- Scissors
- Masking tape
- 4-inch length matching satin ribbon, ⅛ inch wide
- Low-temperature glue gun and glue sticks
- 7¼-inch square white poster board
- 9 matching buttons, ½ inch diameter

1 Measure and mark lines on the foam board with the pencil as shown. Ask an adult to score the lines about ⅛ inch deep with the craft knife. Then run the fabric punch along the scored lines to make them slightly larger.

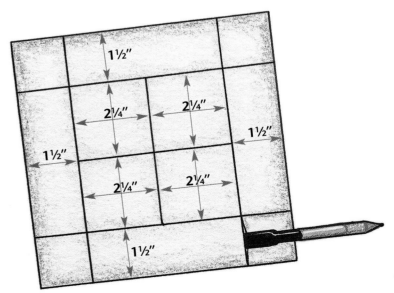

1½″ 2¼″ 2¼″ 1½″ 1½″ 2¼″ 2¼″ 1½″

2 Set a 2¾-inch square of fabric on the foam board, centered over one of the inner squares made by the scored lines. Using the flat side of the fabric punch, carefully poke the fabric into the middle of each of the 4 scored lines of the square to hold the fabric in place. Continue pushing the fabric into the scored lines all the way around the square. Use scissors to snip off any fabric edges that are too long to tuck in. Put the remaining fabric pieces into the foam board in the same way (see the illustration for placement). The outside edges of the 8 pieces of fabric on the sides of the foam board will be loose.

3 Working with the corner pieces first, carefully fold the loose edges of fabric around the back of the foam board and tape them securely. Fold the ribbon in half to form a loop, and glue the two ends to the back of the foam board for a hanger. Glue the poster board onto the back of the foam board so the fabric edges are covered.

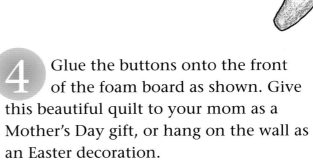

4 Glue the buttons onto the front of the foam board as shown. Give this beautiful quilt to your mom as a Mother's Day gift, or hang on the wall as an Easter decoration.

Bunny Plant Poke

Adult help needed

What You'll Need

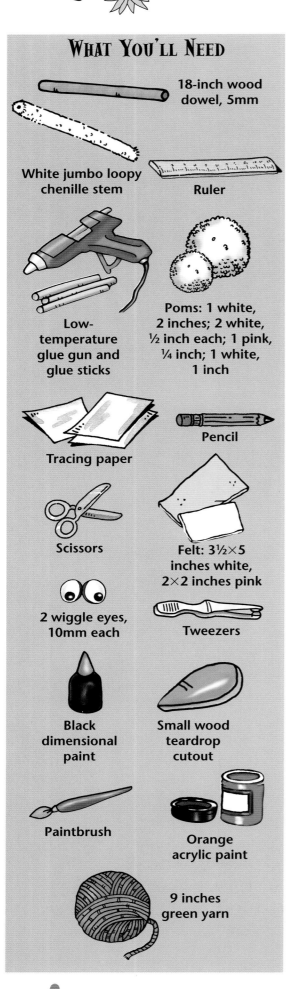

18-inch wood dowel, 5mm

White jumbo loopy chenille stem

Ruler

Low-temperature glue gun and glue sticks

Poms: 1 white, 2 inches; 2 white, ½ inch each; 1 pink, ¼ inch; 1 white, 1 inch

Tracing paper

Pencil

Scissors

Felt: 3½×5 inches white, 2×2 inches pink

2 wiggle eyes, 10mm each

Tweezers

Black dimensional paint

Small wood teardrop cutout

Paintbrush

Orange acrylic paint

9 inches green yarn

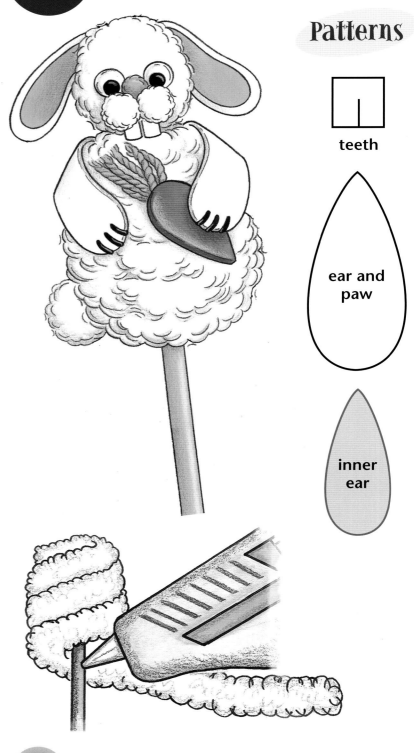

Patterns

teeth

ear and paw

inner ear

1 Spiral-wrap the white chenille stem around 3 inches of one end of the dowel, spot-gluing every inch.

2 For the bunny's head, glue the 2-inch white pom on top of the chenille stem. To make the cheeks, glue two ½-inch white poms side by side toward the bottom of the head. Using the pattern on page 20, trace and cut out the teeth from the white felt; glue just under the cheeks. For the nose, glue the pink pom to the top middle of the cheeks. Use tweezers to glue 2 wiggle eyes above the cheeks.

3 Using the patterns on page 20, trace and cut out 2 white felt ears, 2 pink felt inner ears, and 2 white felt paws. Glue the inner ears to the white ears; glue to the top of the bunny's head. Glue the 1-inch white pom to the bottom left side of the body for the tail. Make toe lines on the bunny's paws with black dimensional paint. Let dry. Glue the paws to the bunny's sides, attaching the points at the neck.

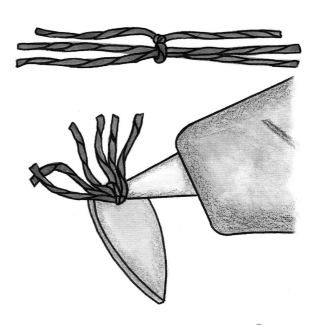

4 Paint the wood teardrop orange; let dry. Cut the green yarn into three 3-inch lengths. For the carrot top, align the ends of two lengths of green yarn and tie the third length around the middle of them. Fold up all the ends and glue the knotted end to the back top of the carrot. Glue the carrot in the bunny's left paw. Insert the dowel into a potted plant for a very bunny Easter decoration!

Maraca Mania

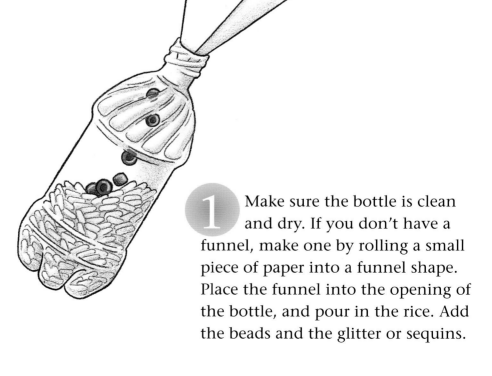

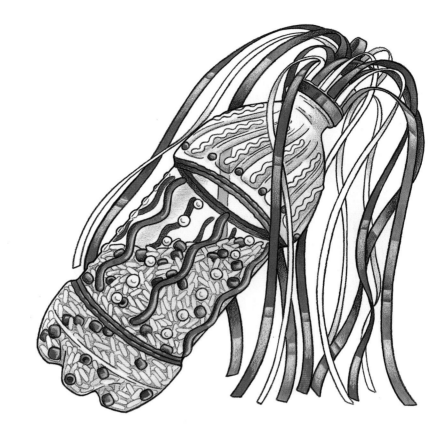

1 Make sure the bottle is clean and dry. If you don't have a funnel, make one by rolling a small piece of paper into a funnel shape. Place the funnel into the opening of the bottle, and pour in the rice. Add the beads and the glitter or sequins.

2 Once you have enough rice, beads, and glitter or sequins in the bottle, spread glue along the edge of the bottle top. Replace the cap, and let the glue dry.

3 Cut a variety of lengths of ribbon, and glue them to the bottle cap or wherever you choose. Use red, white, and green fabric paint to draw designs or write messages on the side of your bottle. When everything is dry, grab the maraca and shake it to make noise for Cinco de Mayo!

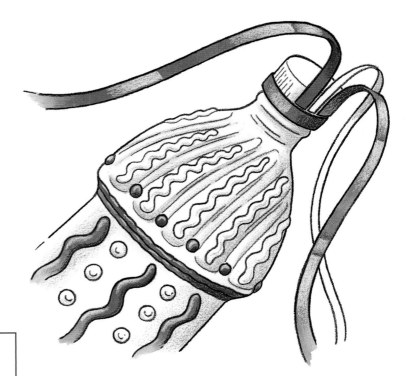

Did You Know?

Cinco de Mayo, which means "Fifth of May" in Spanish, is a holiday to celebrate the Mexican army's victory over the French at the Battle of Puebla on May 5, 1862.

Egg Critter

What You'll Need

- Tracing paper
- Pencil
- Scissors
- 2×3 inches white poster board
- Felt: 2×4 inches orange, ¾×1¼ inches red, 1×2 inches purple
- Low-temperature glue gun and glue sticks
- Orange dimensional paint
- 2-inch yellow plastic egg
- 2-inch yellow pom
- Yarn: 14 inches yellow, 12 inches green
- Ruler
- Tweezers
- 2 wiggle eyes, 10mm each
- Craft feathers (assorted colors): three 4 inches long, two 2 inches long

Adult help needed

Patterns

foot

tongue

beak

bow tie

1 Trace and cut out the foot pattern (above). Make 2 feet out of poster board and 2 out of orange felt. Glue 1 felt foot to 1 poster board foot. Squeeze orange dimensional paint lines on the felt foot according to the pattern; let dry. Repeat for the other foot. Position the feet (felt side up) about ¼ inch apart on your work surface. Glue the yellow plastic egg (rounded side) to the feet.

2 To make the egg critter's head, glue the yellow pom to the top of the egg. For hair, cut five 2-inch lengths of yellow yarn, and align the ends. Wrap the remaining 4-inch length of yellow yarn around the middle of the 2-inch lengths; tie a knot. Fold this piece in half; trim the ends to make them even. Glue the knotted end to the top center of the head. Wrap the middle of the length of green yarn around the bottom of the yarn hairs and tie a bow. Trim the tails.

3 Using the patterns on page 24, trace and cut out the beak from orange felt and the tongue from red felt. Glue the tongue to the inside center of the beak, and fold the beak across the middle as shown on the patterns. Glue the outside of the fold near the bottom of the head. Use tweezers to glue 2 wiggle eyes to the head, just touching the sides of the beak.

4 Use the pattern on page 24 to trace and cut a bow tie from purple felt, and glue it to the egg critter just under the beak. For the tail feathers, glue 4-inch feathers to the lower back of the egg. Glue the 2-inch feathers to the sides of the body for wings.

May "Day-sy" Frame

Adult help needed

WHAT YOU'LL NEED

Wood frame

3 yards lightweight ribbon, ½ inch wide

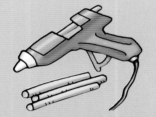

Low-temperature glue gun and glue sticks

Scissors

Pink and white silk daisies

Photo

Heavy-duty clear packing tape (optional)

1 Take apart the wood frame, and set aside the frame backing and the glass. Glue one end of the ribbon to the top middle of the back side of the frame. Wrap the ribbon around the frame, overlapping the ribbon edges to hide the wood. Pull the ribbon taut, but make sure there is enough give so that the frame backing will still fit in the frame.

2 When the frame is completely covered, cut the ribbon and glue the end to the back of the frame.

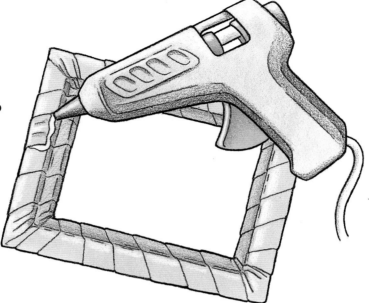

3 Lay the frame right side up on a flat surface. Position the daisies as desired on the front of the frame. Once you're happy with the design, glue the flowers in place.

4 Press the glass back into place, position the photo inside, and fit the frame backing into place. If the backing no longer fits, use heavy-duty clear packing tape to secure the backing to the frame.

Funky Foam Purse

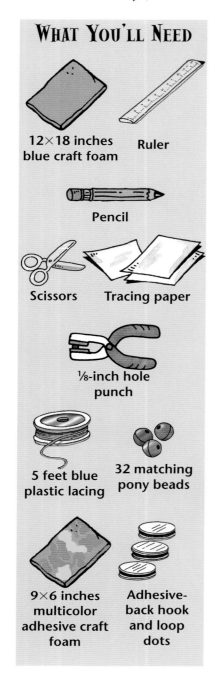

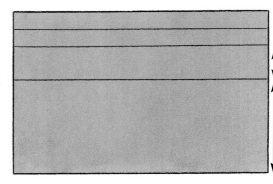

1 Along the shorter edge of the blue foam, measure and mark 2 strips 1¼ inches wide (for the strap) and 1 strip 2½ inches wide. Cut out the strips. Using the pattern on page 30, trace and cut out 2 side panels from the 2½-inch-wide strip (copy the pattern markings). The remaining foam piece should measure about 7 inches wide. This will be for the pouch of the purse. Round the corners of the pouch piece on one side.

1¼"
1¼"
2½"
7"

2 Starting ¼ inch from the squared edge of the pouch piece, measure and mark 26 points ½ inch apart and ¼ inch in from the side edge. Repeat on the other side. Punch holes at all points on all the pieces, including the side panels.

3 Cut a 36-inch length of plastic lacing. Line up the square edge of one side panel with one edge of the pouch piece. Thread the lacing through the first holes of each section, and leave a 10-inch tail on the side panel side. Continue lacing through the matching holes, using a basic sewing stitch, until all the holes are used. Be sure to keep the edges even and leave a 10-inch tail. Repeat on the other side.

4 Thread each tail through the top 2 holes on the side panel (the lace ends should end up on the outside of the side panel). Position one end of a strap piece over the holes at the top of a side panel. Use a pencil to mark points through the punched holes of the side panel to help you punch holes on the strap. Thread one lace end through the top hole on the strap, then thread the same lace diagonally to the bottom hole on the strap. Repeat with the other lace end (lace should have formed an *X*). Thread the lace ends through the opposite bottom strap holes. Tie the ends in a knot. Thread 3 pony beads on the remaining lacing, and tie a double knot on each end to hold the beads in place. Trim excess lacing. Repeat on the other side.

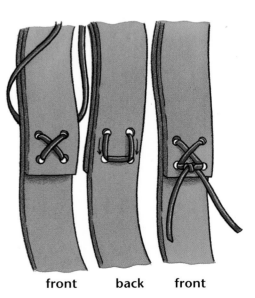

5 Overlap the straps to desired length to fit over your shoulder. Holding the strap pieces in place, punch 4 holes in a square about ½ inch apart and about ¼ inch from the edges of the straps. Cut a 12-inch length of lacing, then thread the lacing down through one bottom hole and up through the other bottom hole. Bring the ends together evenly, cross the lace ends to form an *X*, then thread them down through the top holes. Lace each end back up through the bottom holes, then tie a knot to hold in place. Thread 2 pony beads on each end of the lacing, and tie a double knot on each end to hold the beads in place. Trim excess lacing. Repeat on the other overlapped section of the strap.

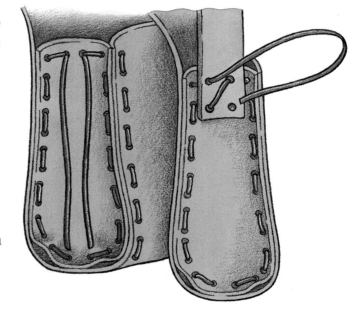

front   back   front

Spring 29

6 Trace and cut out 3 flowers from the multicolor craft foam using the pattern on this page. Copy all markings, and punch holes at the points. Using 4 inches of lacing for each flower, thread the length of lacing through the holes, then tie a knot. Thread 2 pony beads on each end of the lacing, and tie a double knot at each end to hold the beads in place. Remove paper backing and stick the flowers to desired locations on the purse. Remove the paper backing from the loop dots and place them under the purse flap. Press the hook dots on the loop dots, then remove the backing from the hook dots and attach them to the front of the purse.

Patterns

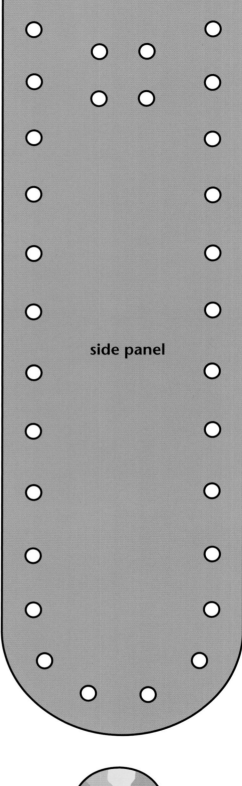

side panel

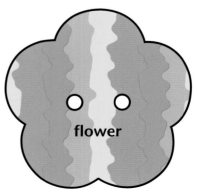

flower

Cool Camp Frame

Adult help needed

WHAT YOU'LL NEED

6½ × 7¼-inch wood frame

Sandpaper

Soft cloth

Acrylic paint

Paintbrushes

Wood craft picks

Scissors

Craft glue

Fine-point permanent markers

Wood craft spoon

Ruler

Waterbase varnish, satin finish

10-inch length ribbon, 1/16 inch (girl only)

Camp photo

CAMP IS FUN!

Whitney!

1 Ask an adult to help you take apart the wood frame, and set aside the frame backing and the glass. Use the sandpaper to remove any rough edges on the wood frame. Wipe the frame with a soft cloth to remove dust, then paint the frame in desired color with paintbrush. Let dry 2 hours.

2 Arrange 13 craft picks on a flat surface for the camp sign, alternating the direction of the picks as shown. Lay 2 craft picks across the sign vertically, and cut off any excess wood. Glue the 2 picks to the sign; let dry 2 hours. Paint the sign desired color. Let dry 1 hour, then use permanent markers to write your name, "Camp is Fun," or anything else you want.

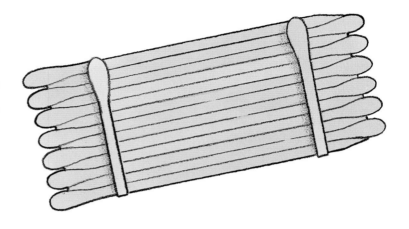

3 To make the head of the boy or girl, measure and cut 1½ inches from the smallest end of the craft spoon. Sand any rough edges. Refer to the illustration to cut craft picks for the hair, ears, and fingers. Paint the head, fingers (if you're making a boy), ears, and hair desired colors. Let dry 1 hour. Glue the hair and ears onto the head to make a boy or girl. Use the the markers to add a face.

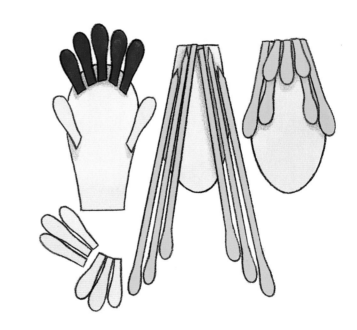

4 Glue the head (and fingers for a boy) to the sign, then glue the sign to the top of the frame. Let dry 2 hours. Paint all the wood with the waterbase varnish. Let dry 1 hour or as directed by the manufacturer. If you're making a girl, tie the ribbon in a bow and glue it to the top of the head. Have an adult help you put the frame back together—be sure to insert a camp photo in the frame to show how much fun you had this summer!

Wingin' It

6-foot length clear
plastic lanyard

24mm split ring

Beads: 26 royal blue baby
pony, 2 black glitter pony,
14 purple glitter pony, 34
light blue baby pony, 22
lavender baby pony, 10
blue glitter pony

Nail clippers

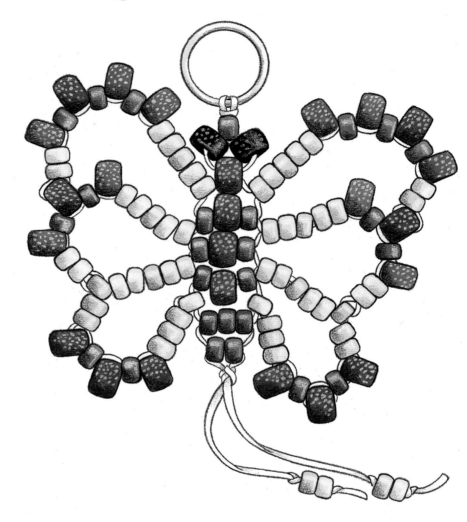

1 Fold the lanyard in half, and slip the looped end through the split ring. Pull the cut ends up through the loop and pull tight. String a royal blue baby pony bead onto the left strand and slide it all the way up. Weave the right strand through the bead from right to left. String 1 black glitter pony bead onto each strand for the eyes, then add 1 purple glitter pony bead to the left strand. Weave the right strand through the purple glitter bead from right to left. Be sure to keep the lanyard flat as you weave it from one row to the next.

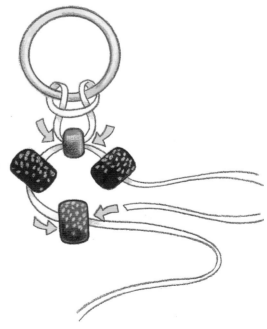

2 To make the first "sidepath" of the right butterfly wing, string beads 1–15 on the right strand. Leave a little space between the beads, and weave back through, skipping the larger beads (beads 12, 10, 8, and 6). Pull tightly as you weave back, allowing the beads to curve as shown. Repeat to make the first sidepath of the left butterfly wing with the left strand. Add 1 royal blue baby pony, 1 purple glitter pony, and 1 royal blue baby pony to the left strand. Weave the right strand through the same 3 beads right to left.

3 String the second sidepath on each side of the butterfly. As you weave back toward the body, make sure to skip bead 15 from the first sidepath. Similarly, after stringing the third sidepath, skip bead 12 from the middle sidepath as you weave back toward the body.

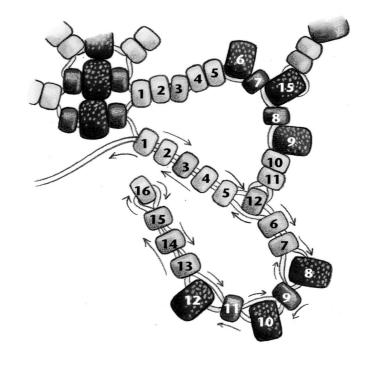

4 Lace the last bead (16) of both lower wings to the body as a bead between rows. Use the bead diagram to finish the last two rows.

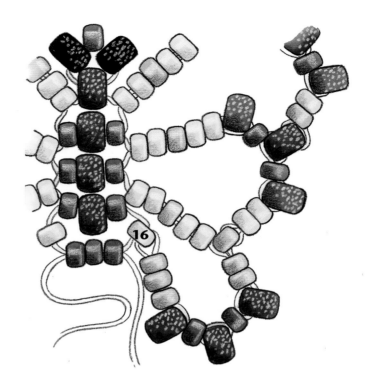

5 Tie the lanyard ends together in an overhand knot. To do this, twist both lanyard ends into a loop and then pull the free ends through the loop. Tie a double knot toward the end of each strand. Thread a lavender bead and a light blue bead on each end, then tie a double knot on each strand to hold the beads in place. Trim excess lanyard with nail clippers, leaving ¼-inch ends.

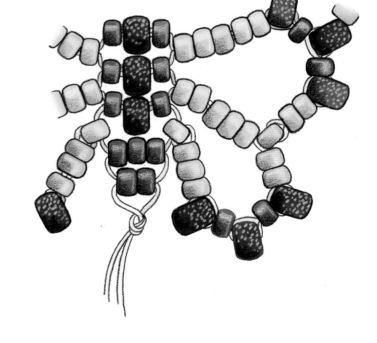

Try This!

Once you have the basic beading techniques down, use different color beads to create all kinds of butterflies. Try making a monarch with orange, black, and white beads.

WHAT YOU'LL NEED

Clean, white T-shirt

Cardboard

Scissors

2 spray bottles

Water

Measuring cup

Red and blue fabric paint, 1 ounce each

Paintbrush

Festive Fireworks T-Shirt

1 Be sure to cover yourself and your work area—this is a very messy project! You may even want to work outside. Cut a piece of cardboard so it fits inside the T-shirt, and slide it inside the shirt. This will prevent the paint from soaking through from one side of the shirt to the other. Lay the shirt flat on your work surface.

2 Add about ⅓ cup of water to each spray bottle. Empty most of the red fabric paint into a spray bottle. Empty most of the blue paint into the other spray bottle. You need to thin the paint just enough so it can be squirted out of the bottle, so you may need to add more water than this (add just a small amount of water at a time).

3 Now for the really fun part! Squirt red and blue starburst designs onto the shirt until it looks the way you want it. Wait for one side to dry (about 1 hour), then flip the shirt over and paint the other side. Let dry.

4 Use a paintbrush and the remaining fabric paint you did not put into the spray bottles to highlight different areas of your design. Let dry. Wear your shirt on the Fourth of July—or any day—with pride! (To care for your shirt, wash it in cold water and hang it up or lay it flat to dry.)

On-the-Go Lap Desk

WHAT YOU'LL NEED

9×12-inch chalkboard

Pencil

Red acrylic paint

Small paintbrush

White paint pen

2-inch-deep plastic container, less than 9×12 inches

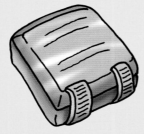

Low-temperature glue gun and glue sticks

1 Use the star stencil in the back of the book to decorate the chalkboard. Trace the star shape on the front of the chalkboard in any design you like.

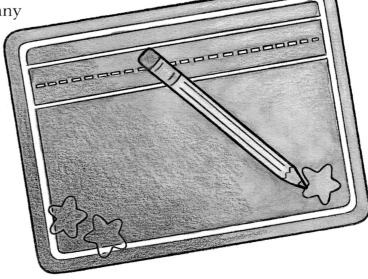

2 Paint the star shapes with the red paint. Let dry, then apply another coat of paint. Add small white detail lines around each star with the paint pen.

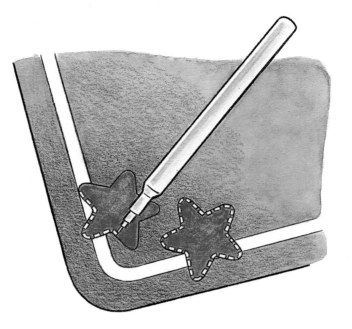

3 Center the chalkboard over the top of the container, then glue in place. Let dry. Fill your lap desk with everything you need for a summer road trip!

Try This!
Instead of a plastic container, you could glue your decorated chalkboard on top of a pillow or a fabric pouch filled with small beans or pellets.

Puffy Paint Caps

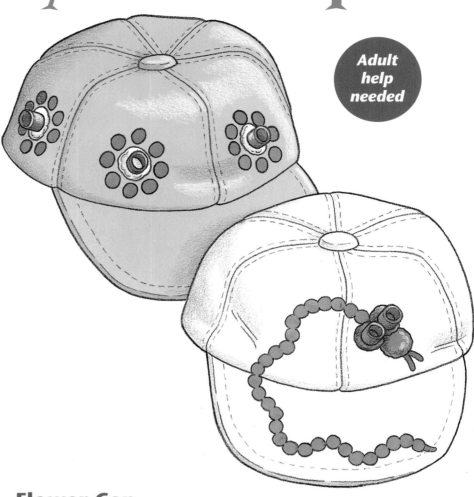

What You'll Need

Plain baseball cap

Foam plates

Fabric paints: velveteen-finish white, matte-finish purple (flower); matte- and velveteen-finish green, velveteen-finish red (snake)

Crayons: 1 jumbo, 1 regular

Paper towels   Iron

4 inches neon pink plastic tubing, ⅜ inch diameter

Scissors   Craft glue

Pencil (snake only)

Toothpicks (snake only)

Flower Cap

1. Pour a small amount of the white and purple fabric paint onto separate foam plates. Use the flat end of a jumbo crayon dipped in velveteen-finish white paint to make dots around the hat for the flowers' centers. Add more paint to the crayon as needed. Wipe off the crayon with a paper towel, and set aside. Make petals by dipping the flat end of a regular crayon into the matte-finish purple paint. Dot 7 or 8 times around each flower center. Let dry 24 hours.

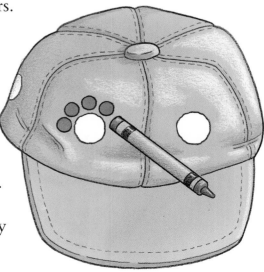

2 Ask an adult to help you use an iron to puff up the velveteen-finish paint. Set the iron on steam, and hold it 1 inch above the surface of those areas that were painted with the velveteen-finish paint until the paint puffs up (do not press the iron to the surface; just let the steam do the work). Let dry 20 minutes. Cut small pieces of plastic tubing and glue them onto the hat for the flowers' centers. Let the glue dry at least 4 hours before wearing.

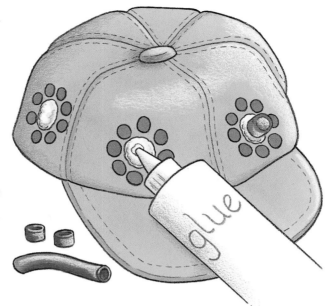

Snake Cap

1 Pour red and both kinds of green paint onto separate plates. Use the pencil to draw a squiggly line on the hat where you want the snake's body to be. Dip the regular-size crayon in the matte-finish green paint, and make dots along the pencil line until you reach the head area. Wipe off the crayon with a paper towel. Make 3 slightly overlapping dots with the jumbo crayon and the velveteen-finish green paint for the head. Wipe off the crayon. Dip the side edge of a toothpick into the red paint, and apply paint onto the hat near the snake's mouth for the tongue. Use another toothpick dipped in the velveteen-finish green to make a tail. Let dry 24 hours.

2 Repeat step 2 of the Flower Cap, this time using the plastic tubing for the snake's eyes.

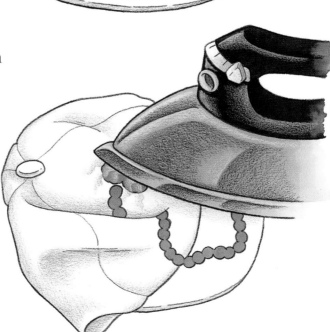

WHAT YOU'LL NEED

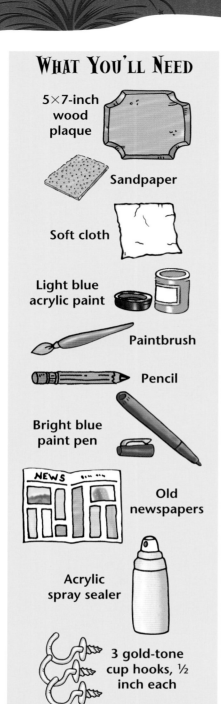

5×7-inch wood plaque

Sandpaper

Soft cloth

Light blue acrylic paint

Paintbrush

Pencil

Bright blue paint pen

Old newspapers

Acrylic spray sealer

3 gold-tone cup hooks, ½ inch each

10 assorted coins, charms, or medallions, between ½ inch and 1½ inches diameter

Low-temperature glue gun and glue sticks

2 soda can tabs

Adult help needed

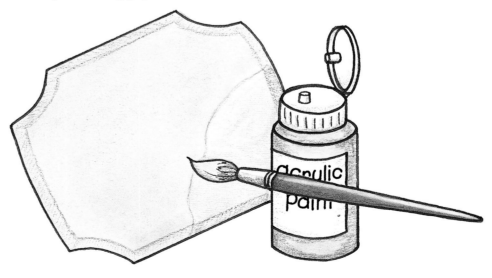

1 Lightly sand the wood plaque; wipe it clean with a soft cloth. Paint the surface with light blue paint. Let dry, then apply a second coat.

2 Using a pencil, lightly print the words "Dad's Keys" on the plaque. Trace the pencil lines with the paint pen. (Hint: Add small dots to the beginning and end of each letter for a fun style.) If the plaque has a raised edge, outline the edge with the paint marker. Place the plaque outside on old newspapers. Ask an adult to help you lightly spray the plaque with the acrylic spray sealer. Let dry.

3 Ask an adult to help you screw the 3 cup hooks into the wood, evenly spaced, about 1 inch up from the bottom of the plaque. Arrange the assorted coins, charms, or medallions on the plaque. When you're happy with the design, glue them in place.

4 To hang the plaque, glue 2 soda can tabs to the back of the plaque so the loops of the tabs will hang on nails in the wall. Give to your dad on Father's Day or any time of year!

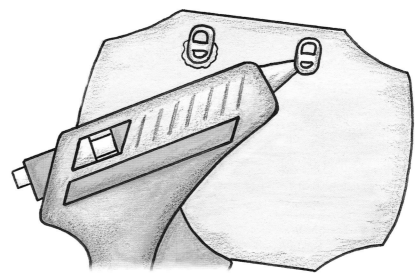

Funtime Flip-Flops

Adult help needed

WHAT YOU'LL NEED

Foam flip-flops

2-yard-length grosgrain or woven ribbon, 2 inches wide

Scissors

Low-temperature glue gun and glue sticks

2 plastic or silk flowers (about 1 to 2 inches diameter) or 2 small plastic frogs

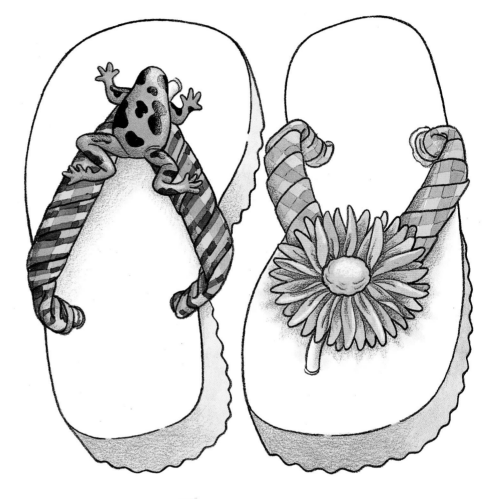

1 Cut the ribbon into two equal lengths. Loosen one side of a flip-flop thong by pushing it down through the bottom of the shoe. Ask an adult to help you use the tip of the scissors to poke the end of one length of ribbon through the hole on one side. Pull the ribbon so about 1 inch hangs underneath the flip-flop. Using the glue gun, fill the hole with glue, then pull the thong up so it fits back into the hole on the bottom. Make sure the end of the ribbon is still visible from the bottom of the shoe.

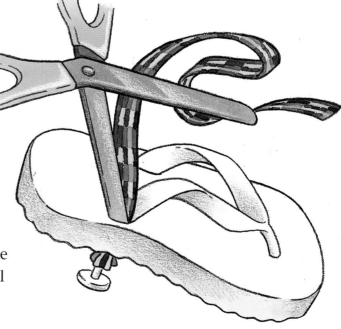

2 Working on the top of the flip-flop, wrap the ribbon around the thong so the plastic is completely covered. Overlap the edges of the ribbon each time you wrap it around to make sure it's secure. When you reach the other side of the thong, secure the end of the ribbon through the hole in the bottom of the flip-flop as you did in step 1.

3 If you are making flower flip-flops, trim the stems from the plastic flowers. Using the glue gun, attach the flower or frog in the center of thong. Repeat all steps for the other flip-flop.

Try This!

Don't stop with frogs or flowers! You can make all kinds of fun flip-flops using plastic bugs, cute erasers, or whatever else you dream up!

High-Flying Kite

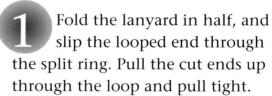

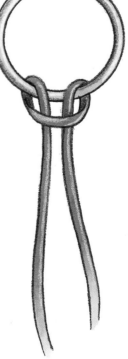

1 Fold the lanyard in half, and slip the looped end through the split ring. Pull the cut ends up through the loop and pull tight.

2 String a light blue bead onto the left strand and slide it all the way up. Weave the right strand through the bead from right to left. Now slide 3 light blue beads onto the left strand. Weave the right strand through the beads from right to left.

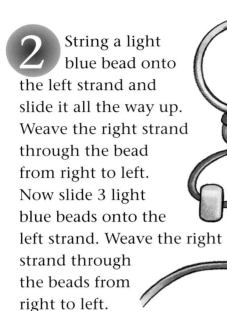

3 Keep stringing and weaving in this manner, following the diagram. Be sure to pull the cords firmly and to keep the lanyard flat as you weave each row.

4 Finish the body of the kite by tying both lanyard ends in an overhand knot. To do this, twist both lanyard ends into a loop and then pull the free ends through the loop. Tie a second overhand knot about ½ inch from the first, then string 1 red bead on each strand of lanyard followed by another overhand knot—this creates the "bows" that weight the tail of the kite. Repeat this process to make 2 more bows with yellow and light blue beads. Use nail clippers to trim the excess lanyard, leaving a ½-inch tail.

WHAT YOU'LL NEED

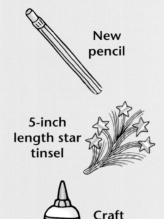

New pencil

5-inch length star tinsel

Craft glue

Felt: 2¾×¾ inches royal blue, 1½×5 inches white, seven ⅛×6-inch red strips

White acrylic paint

Toothpick

Pen

1 Glue one end of the length of star tinsel to the metal part of the pencil eraser. Fold the tinsel over the top of the eraser, forming a loop, and glue down the other end of the tinsel.

2 Using a toothpick, dot white acrylic paint onto the royal blue felt to make stars (about 3 rows, 10 dots in each row). Set aside to dry for 30 minutes.

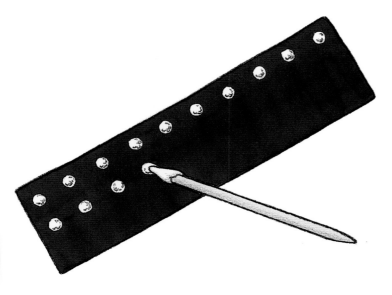

3 Fold the white felt in half lengthwise, bringing the shortest ends together. Use the pen to mark the halfway point on the inside of the fold. Unfold the felt and lay it flat with the unmarked side facing up. Glue a red felt strip along the top edge of the white felt piece. Repeat with the other red strips, leaving a little bit of space between the strips so the white felt looks striped. Let dry 30 minutes.

4 Turn over the white felt. Apply glue to the back side, then lay the pencil over the ink mark at the halfway point. Fold both sides of the felt around the pencil, covering up the end of the tinsel and any metal part of the eraser that is still showing. Matching the ends of the white felt, press firmly to hold.

5 Glue the royal blue felt piece in the upper left corner of flag, wrapping the end around to the opposite side. Press firmly to secure.

Adult help needed

What You'll Need

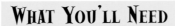

6×9-inch chalkboard

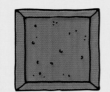
Red acrylic paint

Paintbrush

Tracing paper

Pencil

Scissors

Craft foam: purple, blue, green

White paint pen

18-inch length grosgrain ribbon, ¾ inch wide

Low-temperature glue gun and glue sticks

Chalk

1 Paint the chalkboard frame red. Let dry, then apply another coat.

2 Using the patterns below, trace and cut out the turtle from purple craft foam, the seahorse from blue foam, and the alligator from green craft foam. (You may want to use transfer paper to get the pattern details.) Add details on the front of each sea creature with the white paint pen. Let dry.

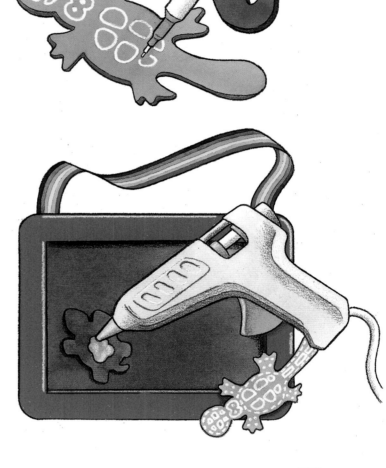

3 Glue one end of the ribbon to each side of the chalkboard at the top. Position the sea creatures on the front of the chalkboard around the frame; glue in place. Use chalk to write a message on your board, then hang it on your bedroom door to let friends and family know if you are in, out, or just want to be left alone!

Patterns

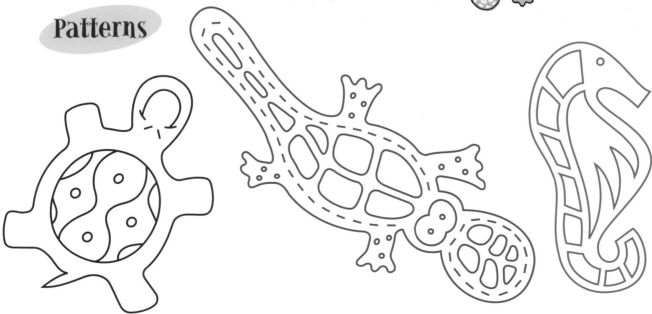

Super Summer Visors

Plastic visor: green (frog), yellow (sunflower)

Tracing paper

Pencil

Scissors

Craft foam: green, white, black, red (frog); yellow (sunflower)

Glue

GLUE

Fabric paint: black, green (frog); red, yellow (sunflower)

Fabric Paint

frog eye/ tongue

Frog Visor

1 Trace and cut 2 large frog eye shapes out of green craft foam, using the pattern on this page. Put a little glue along the straight edge of each cutout, and glue the foam to the top edge of the green visor.

glue

2 Cut 2 circles out of the white craft foam and 2 smaller circles out of the black craft foam. Glue each white circle to each green frog eye shape. Glue the black circles onto the white circles.

3 Make 2 nostrils on the visor with the black fabric paint. Outline the green of each eye with green fabric paint. Use the pattern on page 52 to make a tongue shape out of the red craft foam. Glue the tongue along the curved edge of the visor.

Sunflower Visor

1 Using the pattern below, trace and cut 9 petal shapes from the yellow craft foam. Glue them along the underside of the curved edge of the yellow visor.

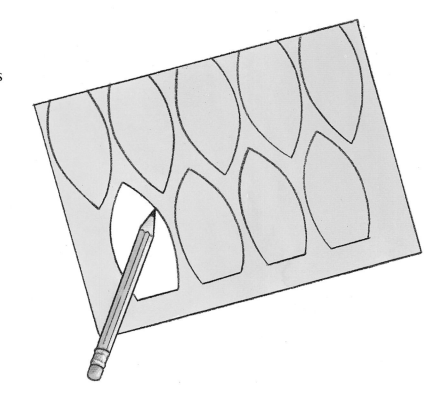

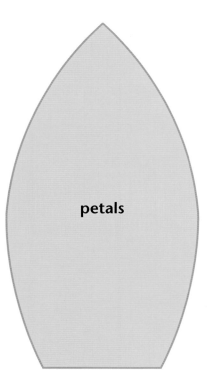

petals

2 Use the red fabric paint to add little marks on the visor to resemble sunflower seeds. You can also use yellow fabric paint to outline the bottom edge of the petals.

Totally Buggy Clips

1 Using the stencils in the back of the book, trace and cut out bug shapes in various colors of craft foam.

2 To make a ladybug, glue 2 ladybug wings on top of a ladybug body, keeping the wings slightly apart in the middle. Use the hole punch to make small circles out of craft foam; glue them to the top of the ladybug wings. For the butterfly and dragonfly, glue a body cutout to a wing cutout. Let dry.

3 Turn the bugs over, and glue a clothespin to the back of each bug. Let dry. String the fishing line along a wall and secure it with a thumbtack on each end. Clip your buggy clothespins onto the line to hang your very best photos and artwork!

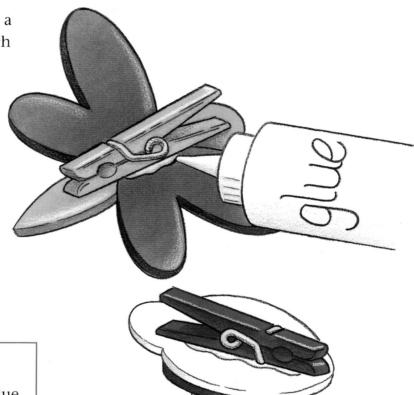

Try This!

Instead of mini clothespins, glue the buggy foam shapes onto adhesive-back magnet strips. Then hang your best artwork or top-notch tests on the refrigerator for all to see!

What You'll Need

Brown grocery bag (6½×10-inch base, at least 12 inches high)

Ruler

 Pencil

Pinking shears

Tracing paper

Scissors

Shiny paper: 9×9 inches white, 9×9 inches orange, 2×3 inches yellow, 2×2 inches green, 2×3 inches black

 Glue stick

Black felt-point permanent marker

1½×18-inch white poster board strip

Low-temperature glue gun and glue sticks

 52-inch length Halloween print craft ribbon, 1½ inches wide

 2 sheets black tissue paper

Trick-or-Treat Bag

Adult help needed

 Use the ruler and pencil to measure and mark the paper bag to 12 inches high. Cut along mark with the pinking shears.

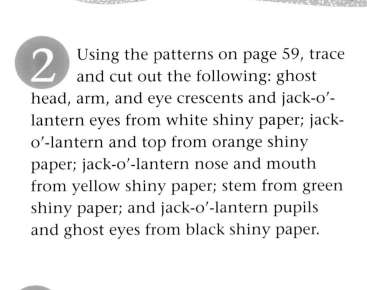

2 Using the patterns on page 59, trace and cut out the following: ghost head, arm, and eye crescents and jack-o'-lantern eyes from white shiny paper; jack-o'-lantern and top from orange shiny paper; jack-o'-lantern nose and mouth from yellow shiny paper; stem from green shiny paper; and jack-o'-lantern pupils and ghost eyes from black shiny paper.

3 Referring to the illustration, position the parts on your work surface in the following order: ghost head and arm; jack-o'-lantern top, stem, head, eyes, pupils, nose, and mouth; and ghost eyes and eye crescents. Use the glue stick to assemble. Draw the eyebrows and mouth on the ghost and the eyebrows on the pumpkin with the black marker. Use the glue stick to attach the entire jack-o'-lantern/ghost piece to the front of the bag.

4 To make the handle, use a glue gun to attach 1 inch of the poster board strip to the top outside middle of the short side of the bag. Repeat on the other side of the bag with the other end of the poster board strip. Glue one end of the ribbon to the middle of the bottom of the bag, spot-gluing as you go up the side of the bag, across the poster board strip, down the other side, and across the bottom until the ribbon overlaps the other end. Tuck 2 sheets of black tissue paper inside the bag, and fill with Halloween treats!

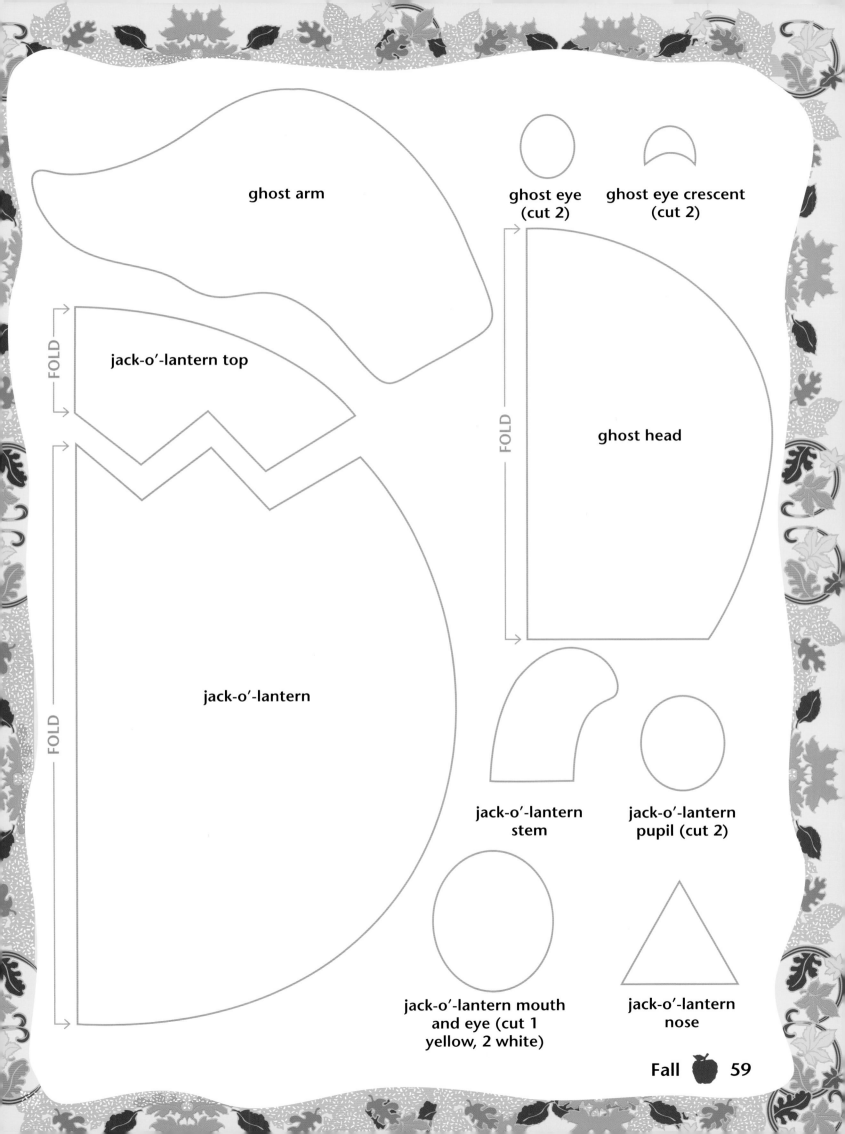

ghost arm

ghost eye
(cut 2)

ghost eye crescent
(cut 2)

FOLD

jack-o'-lantern top

FOLD

ghost head

jack-o'-lantern

jack-o'-lantern
stem

jack-o'-lantern
pupil (cut 2)

FOLD

jack-o'-lantern mouth
and eye (cut 1
yellow, 2 white)

jack-o'-lantern
nose

Rainbow Pencil Holder

Adult help needed

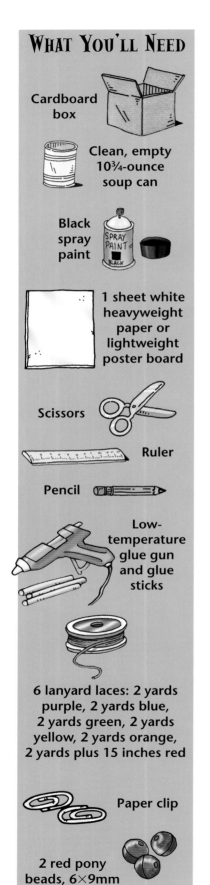

WHAT YOU'LL NEED

Cardboard box

Clean, empty 10¾-ounce soup can

Black spray paint

1 sheet white heavyweight paper or lightweight poster board

Scissors

Ruler

Pencil

Low-temperature glue gun and glue sticks

6 lanyard laces: 2 yards purple, 2 yards blue, 2 yards green, 2 yards yellow, 2 yards orange, 2 yards plus 15 inches red

Paper clip

2 red pony beads, 6×9mm

1 Place the cardboard box on your covered work surface, and place the soup can inside the box. (You may want to complete this step outside or in the garage.) With an adult's help, spray-paint the inside, bottom, and rims of the can with black spray paint. Let dry.

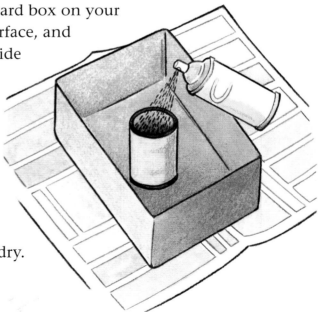

2 Cut the paper or poster board to fit around the can. Measure six ⅝-inch horizontal sections on the paper, and draw lines with the pencil to divide the sections. Glue the paper around the can with the lines on the outside.

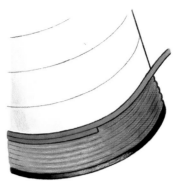

4 To start the next color, glue one end of the blue lace next to the purple lace end. Tightly wrap the blue lace around the can 7 or 8 times to the next ⅝-inch mark. Cut and glue the lace end to the back of the can. Repeat to wrap the can with the green, yellow, orange, and red lanyard laces. Before you finish wrapping the red lanyard, straighten out the end of the paper clip, and place it at the top of the can. Wrap the last 3 red lace wraps over the paper clip.

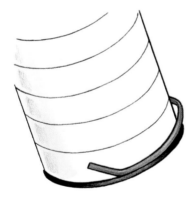

3 Angle and glue the end of the purple lanyard along the bottom of the can. Begin wrapping the purple lace tightly around the can, covering the glued lace end. Keep the lace flat as you work. Tightly wrap the can 7 or 8 times until you reach the first ⅝-inch mark. At the back of the can, cut any excess lace and glue the lace end to the can.

5 Insert the end of the red lanyard through the last 3 wraps, remove the paper clip, and pull the lace tight. Glue the end in place, and trim any excess lanyard. Tie the 15-inch length of red lanyard into a bow. Thread a red pony bead on each lace end, and tie a knot under each bead. Glue the bow to the front of the can.

Witch's Necklace

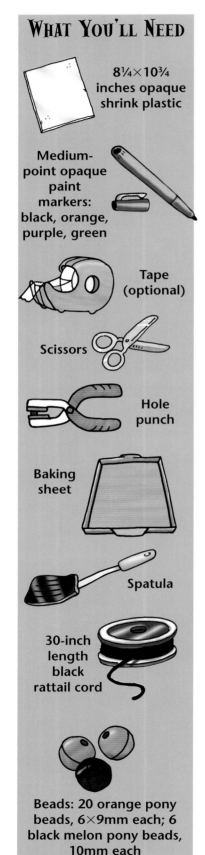

8¼×10¾ inches opaque shrink plastic

Medium-point opaque paint markers: black, orange, purple, green

Tape (optional)

Scissors

Hole punch

Baking sheet

Spatula

30-inch length black rattail cord

Beads: 20 orange pony beads, 6×9mm each; 6 black melon pony beads, 10mm each

Adult help needed

1 Using the patterns on page 64, trace the ghost, bat, and witch outlines onto the shrink plastic with the black paint marker. You may want to tape the shrink plastic on top of the patterns to hold the plastic in place.

2 Trace the faces and other details from the patterns onto the shapes with the paint markers, using the colors shown. Use a smooth back-and-forth motion when you color so you cover the shrink plastic evenly. Let each color dry completely before adding the next color. (Opaque plastic will appear white when it shrinks, so you don't have to color any areas that should be white.) When the paint is dry, cut out each shape along its outline. Use the hole punch to make 2 holes in each shape as indicated on the patterns.

3 Ask an adult to help you bake the shapes in the oven according to the manufacturer's directions. (Note: Do not remove the shapes from the oven until they have completely flattened. Use a spatula to separate them if the parts stick to each other while baking and to press them after you take them out of the oven.) When the shapes are done baking, remove them from the oven and let them cool.

4 Insert one end of the rattail cord through the holes on the witch's hat and slide the witch to the middle of the cord. (Hold the two ends of the cord together in one hand and pull on the witch with the other hand to make sure it is in the middle, and keep it in the middle as you work.) Slide 2 orange beads, 1 black bead, and 2 more orange beads onto the cord on the right side of the witch. Slide the ghost onto the cord on the right side of the beads, then add 2 orange beads, 1 black bead, 2 orange beads, 1 black bead, and 2 orange beads onto the cord on the right side of the ghost. Tie a knot in the cord to the right of the last bead.

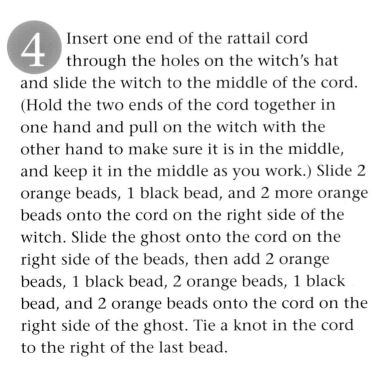

5 Slide 2 orange beads, 1 black bead, and 2 orange beads onto the cord on the left side of the witch. Slide the bat onto the cord on the left side of the beads, then slide 2 orange beads, 1 black bead, 2 orange beads, 1 black bead, and 2 orange beads onto the cord on the left side of the bat. Tie a knot in the cord to the left of the last bead. Tie the ends of the cord together to finish the necklace.

Patterns

bat

ghost

witch

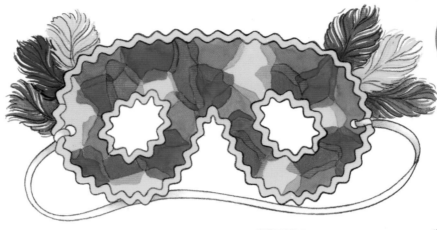

Adult help needed

What You'll Need

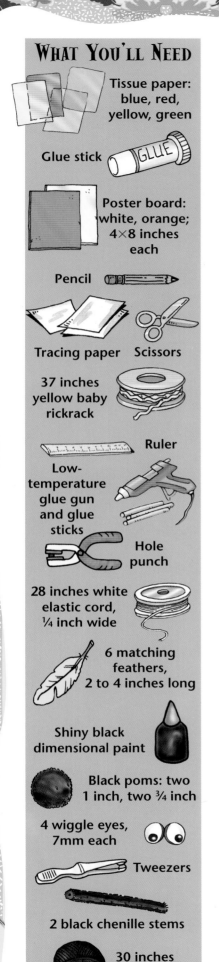

Tissue paper: blue, red, yellow, green

Glue stick

Poster board: white, orange; 4×8 inches each

Pencil

Tracing paper   Scissors

37 inches yellow baby rickrack

Ruler

Low-temperature glue gun and glue sticks

Hole punch

28 inches white elastic cord, ¼ inch wide

6 matching feathers, 2 to 4 inches long

Shiny black dimensional paint

Black poms: two 1 inch, two ¾ inch

4 wiggle eyes, 7mm each

Tweezers

2 black chenille stems

30 inches black yarn

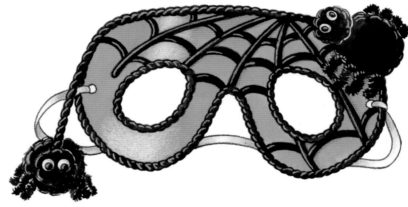

Feather Mask

1 Rip the tissue paper into irregular ½-inch to 1¼-inch pieces. Attach the ripped pieces to the white poster board with the glue stick, overlapping the edges and randomly placing the colors until the entire poster board is covered. Turn over the poster board. Trace and cut out the mask outline and eye holes from the poster board using the pattern on page 66.

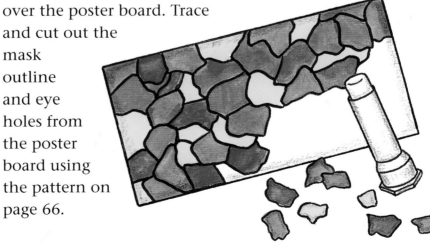

2 With the mask right side up, attach 5 inches of rickrack, a few inches at a time, around each eye hole with the glue gun. Glue the remaining 27-inch length of rickrack around the outside edge of the mask. Punch a hole on each side of the mask as indicated on the pattern. Insert the ends of a 14-inch length of elastic through the holes, and tie knots at the back of the mask (adjust as needed to fit your head). Spot-glue elastic knots to hold. Use the glue gun to attach the ends of 3 feathers to the back top of the mask on each side.

Spider Mask

1 Trace and cut out the mask outline and eye holes from the orange poster board using the pattern below. Punch holes on each side of the mask as indicated on the pattern.

2 Lightly draw pencil web guidelines on the front of the mask according to the pattern. Squeeze dimensional paint on the web lines; let dry.

3 Glue a 1-inch and ¾-inch black pom together to make a spider's head and body. Use the tweezers to glue 2 wiggle eyes to the front of the head. For legs, stack and glue the middles of four 3-inch lengths of chenille stems. Glue the body to the top of the leg stack. Bend the end of each leg down ½ inch. Bend out ¼ inch on the end for the foot, and slightly flatten out legs. Repeat to make another spider, but do not flatten out the legs.

4 Leaving 2 inches unglued, begin gluing a 22-inch length of yarn about ½ inch above the left hole punch, continuing all the way around the outside of the mask. Glue the dangling end of yarn between a spider's head and body pom. Cut the remaining length of yarn in half, and glue each length around an eye hole. Glue the second spider to the upper right side of the mask. Attach the elastic cord as explained in step 2 of the Feather Mask.

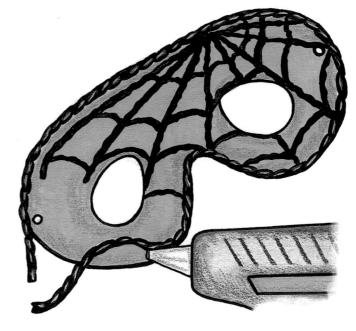

Veggie Magnets

What You'll Need

10×10 inches adhesive-back shelf paper

Tape

20 wood craft picks, 3½ inches long each

Ruler

Pencil

Scissors

Acrylic paint: brown, orange, green, yellow, white

Paintbrushes

4 mini wood craft sticks, ⅜×2½ inches each

Fine-point permanent markers: black, red

8 wiggle eyes, 5mm

Tweezers

Craft glue

½×2½-inch strip adhesive-back magnet

1 Remove the backing from the shelf paper and place it onto a flat surface with the adhesive side up. Use tape to hold down the corners. Measure and mark ½ inch from the pointed ends of 5 craft picks. Cut each pick at the marking. Place the pointed pieces on the shelf paper to hold while painting. Paint 4 pointed pieces brown for the onion roots and 1 piece orange for the tip of the carrot. Lay all the remaining craft picks and sticks on the shelf paper, leaving a little space between each piece. Paint all the remaining craft picks green. Refer to the illustration to paint the mini craft sticks for each vegetable. Let dry 1 hour, then turn over and paint the back sides. Let dry 1 hour.

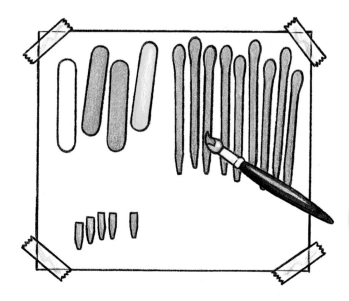

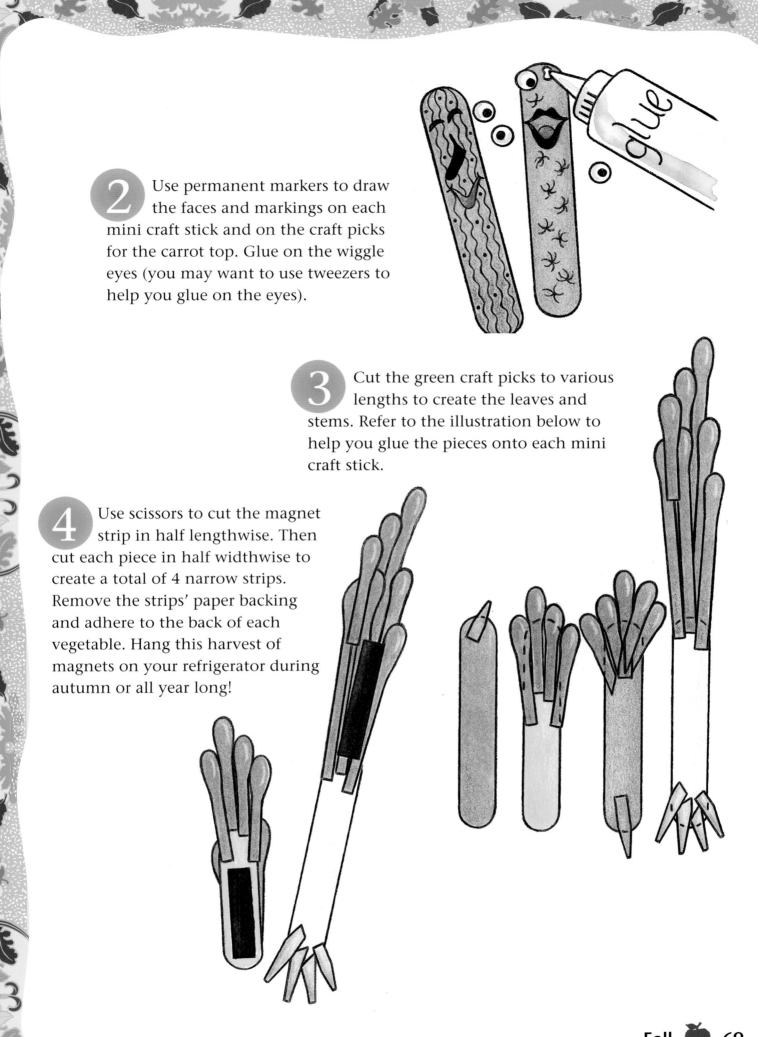

2 Use permanent markers to draw the faces and markings on each mini craft stick and on the craft picks for the carrot top. Glue on the wiggle eyes (you may want to use tweezers to help you glue on the eyes).

3 Cut the green craft picks to various lengths to create the leaves and stems. Refer to the illustration below to help you glue the pieces onto each mini craft stick.

4 Use scissors to cut the magnet strip in half lengthwise. Then cut each piece in half widthwise to create a total of 4 narrow strips. Remove the strips' paper backing and adhere to the back of each vegetable. Hang this harvest of magnets on your refrigerator during autumn or all year long!

Handmade Paper

WHAT YOU'LL NEED

- 5×7-inch wood picture frame
- 8×10 inches coarse nylon net
- Staple gun and staples
- 1-gallon bucket
- Large brown paper grocery bag
- Large slotted spoon
- Blender
- Deep plastic dishpan
- 21×21 inches old sheet
- 20×20 inches flat, smooth, or nonporous plastic or similar material
- Sponge
- Clothesline and clothespins

Adult help needed

1 Ask an adult to help you staple the nylon net across the back of the picture frame, stretching the net tightly. Set aside. Fill a bucket halfway with warm water. Tear the grocery bag into 2-inch squares. Drop the pieces into the bucket of water and stir with the slotted spoon. Let soak ½ hour.

2 Add the soaked paper to the blender with an equal amount of water a little at a time. Don't overload the blender, and use plenty of water. Have an adult help you blend the paper on low speed, then medium speed until it becomes pulpy. Don't overblend. Fill the dishpan halfway with warm water. Pour the pulp into the pan.

3 Hold the frame horizontally, net side up. As you lower it into the pan of pulp, tilt it down and scoop under the pulp, moving it away from your body. Tilt it horizontally under the water and lift up, shaking it slightly. Do this in one smooth, continuous motion. If the pulp is too lumpy or has holes, dump it back into the pan and start over.

4 Let the pulp on the frame drain for a moment over the pan. Wet the sheet and smooth it onto the flat plastic, removing any air bubbles. It's important that the sheet be flat and stuck to the surface; if not, the pulp will not come off the netting later. Turn the frame with the pulp upside down and set it onto the wet sheet. Use a sponge to press out as much water as possible. Do not rub. When most of the water has been removed, lift the frame away from the pulp. The pulp should stick to the sheet. If it does not stick or if there are holes, dump it back into the pan of pulp and start over.

5 Once the pulp is stuck to the sheet, pin the sheet to the clothesline until the piece of paper on it is dry. Then carefully peel away the paper. Make more pieces and put them together to make a notebook, or use your handmade paper for writing notes. You could also make a fall collage on the paper with real leaves or leaf cutouts (see the leaf stencils in the back of this book for ideas).

Turkey Table Favor

Adult help needed

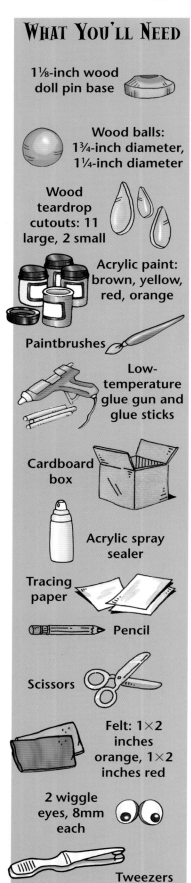
1 Paint all the wood pieces in the following colors: doll pin base, 1¾-inch ball, and 1¼-inch ball—brown; 4 large teardrops—yellow; 4 large teardrops—red; 3 large teardrops and 2 small teardrops—orange. Let dry, then apply a second coat of paint. Let dry completely.

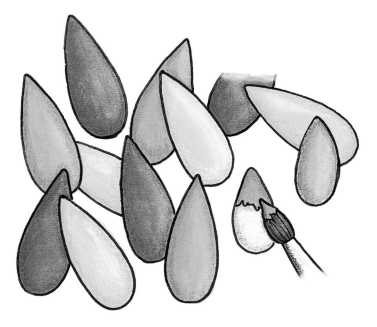

2 To make the turkey's body, glue the 1¾-inch ball to the doll pin base. For the head, glue the 1¼-inch wood ball to the front top of the body.

3 Arrange the large teardrop pieces as shown in the illustration for the turkey's feathers. Overlap the edges of the teardrops and glue them together so they form a half circle of feathers. Glue the half circle of feathers to the body at the center and at each end of the half circle. To make the wings, glue a small teardrop to each side of the body. Put the turkey in a cardboard box in a well-ventilated area, and have an adult help you lightly spray it with acrylic sealer. Let dry.

4 To make the beak, use the pattern below to trace and cut out 2 triangles from the orange felt. Align the short sides of each triangle and glue them to the center front of the head. Use the pattern below to trace and cut out the wattle from the red felt. Glue the top of the wattle to the head just below the beak. Glue the wiggle eyes to the turkey's head above the beak (you may want to use tweezers to help you with this).

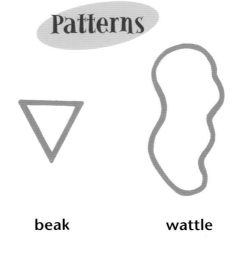

Patterns

beak   wattle

WHAT YOU'LL NEED

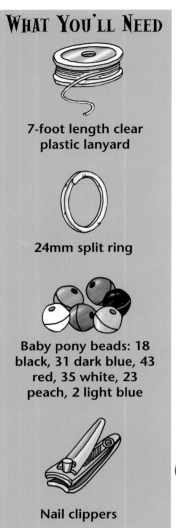

7-foot length clear plastic lanyard

24mm split ring

Baby pony beads: 18 black, 31 dark blue, 43 red, 35 white, 23 peach, 2 light blue

Nail clippers

Hip, Hip, Hooray Cheerleader

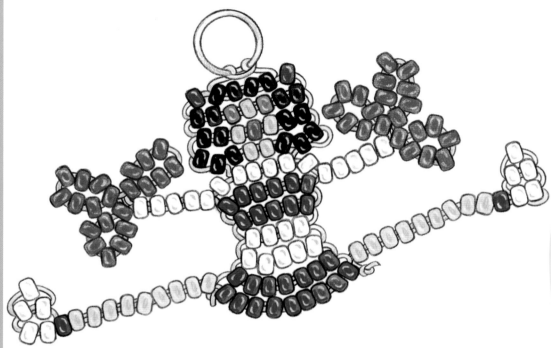

1 Fold the lanyard in half, and slip the looped end through the split ring. Pull the cut ends up through the loop and pull tight. Begin at the top of the cheerleader's head by stringing 4 black baby pony beads onto the left strand. Weave the right strand through the beads from right to left. Add 1 dark blue baby pony bead to each strand. Follow the diagram on the right to string and weave the next 2 rows of beads, counting the beads out carefully as the colors change to create the cheerleader's face and hair. Be sure to pull the cords firmly and to keep the lanyard flat as you weave each row. When you get to the fourth row, string beads onto the left strand according to the diagram, and weave the right strand back through all the beads. Now weave the left strand through the second black bead from the left and the right strand through the second black bead from the right.

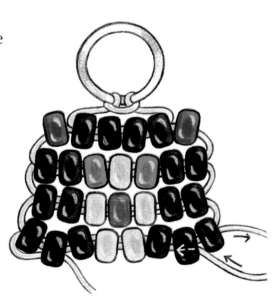

2 For the fifth row, or the cheerleader's arms, start by stringing and weaving 4 white baby pony beads. Add 6 white pony beads to the right strand, then make 3 "sidepaths" with red beads for the cheerleader's pom-poms. To make a sidepath, string on beads 1–7. Leave a little space between the beads, and weave back through bead 1. Pull tightly as you weave back, allowing the beads to curve as shown. Repeat for other 2 sidepaths, then weave the strand back through the last 5 white beads. Repeat for the left arm and pom-pom with the left strand.

3 Continue weaving and stringing rows 6–10 according to the diagram at the bottom of this page. When you get to row 11, or the legs, string 9 dark blue baby pony beads onto the left strand; weave the right strand back through the beads. Now string 9 peach beads and 1 dark blue bead on the right strand. Make a foot by stringing on beads 1–5. Leave a little space between the beads, and weave back through beads 3, 4, 1, and 2 (allow the beads to curve as shown). Weave back through bead 1 again, then weave the strand through the last dark blue pony bead and 9 peach beads. Repeat for the other leg and foot.

4 Finish by twisting each lanyard end into a loop and then pull the free end through the loop. Trim any excess lanyard with the nail clippers.

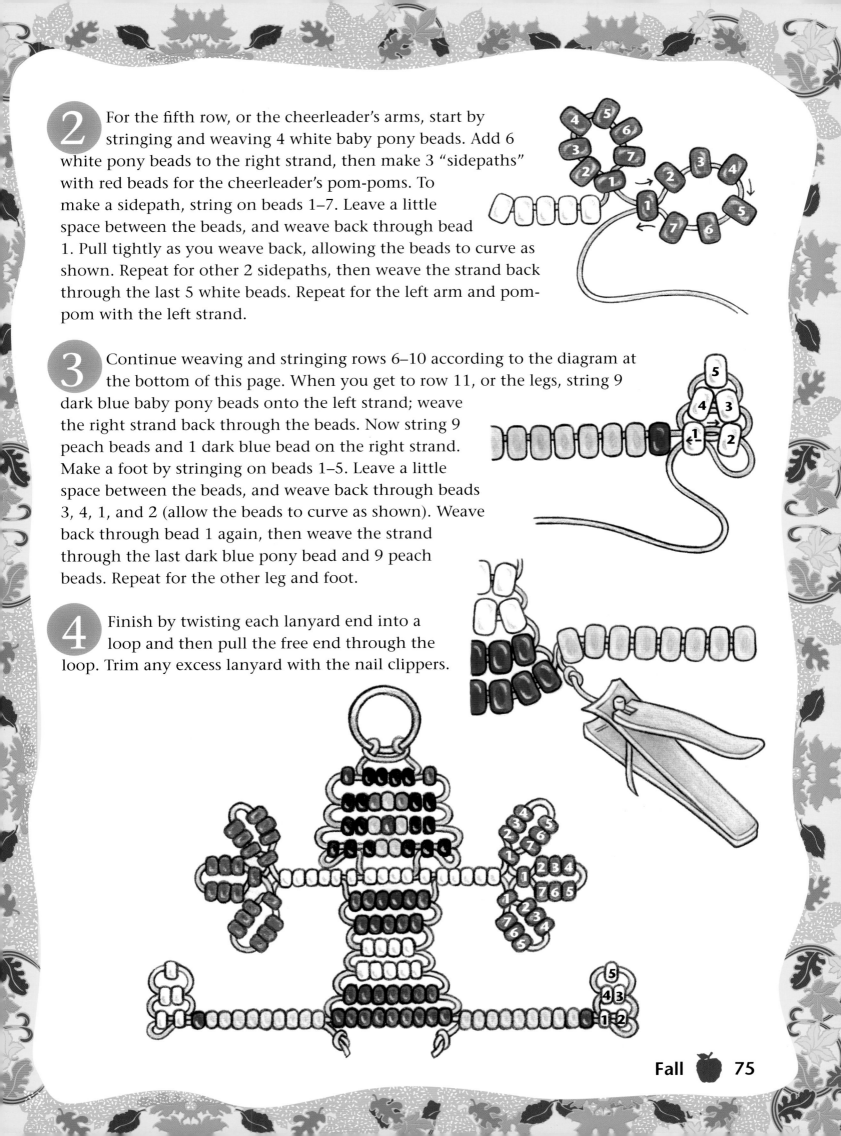

Halloween Mobile

WHAT YOU'LL NEED

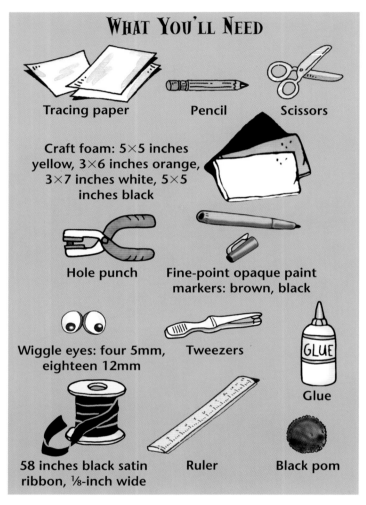

Tracing paper   Pencil   Scissors

Craft foam: 5×5 inches
yellow, 3×6 inches orange,
3×7 inches white, 5×5
inches black

Hole punch   Fine-point opaque paint
markers: brown, black

Wiggle eyes: four 5mm,   Tweezers
eighteen 12mm

GLUE

Glue

58 inches black satin
ribbon, ⅛-inch wide   Ruler   Black pom

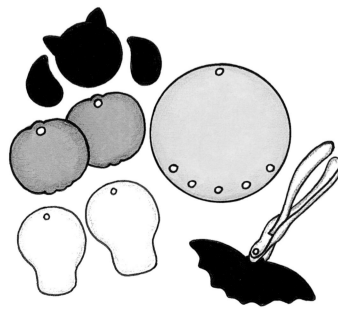

1 Using the patterns on page 78, trace and cut out the following shapes from the craft foam: 1 yellow moon, 2 orange pumpkins (one of each outline), 2 white skulls, 1 black bat, 1 black cat head, and 2 black cat paws. Use the hole punch to make holes in the foam shapes as shown on the patterns.

2 Draw lines on both sides of the pumpkins with the brown marker; use the black marker to make faces on both sides. Let dry. Draw faces on both sides of the skulls with the black marker; let dry. Use tweezers to glue two 5mm eyes on both sides of the bat. Glue two 12mm eyes on both sides of the pumpkins and skulls.

3 Cut a 12-inch length of ribbon. Insert one end of the ribbon 1½ inches into the single hole at the top of the moon. Tie a double knot in the ribbon to securely attach it to the moon. Trim the short end of the ribbon close to the knot. Position and glue the cat head on the back upper side of the moon. Position and glue the cat paws on the front of the moon, with the right paw covering the ribbon hanger. Glue the black pom nose on the cat head so it slightly overlaps the edge of the moon, and glue two 12mm eyes to the cat head.

4 Cut the remaining ribbon into the following lengths, and use double knots to tie one end of each length to a foam shape and the other end to a hole at the bottom of the moon: 6-inch length for 1 pumpkin, 9-inch length for 1 skull, 13-inch length for the bat; 11-inch length for 1 pumpkin, 7-inch length for 1 skull. Trim the ends of each length of ribbon close to the knots.

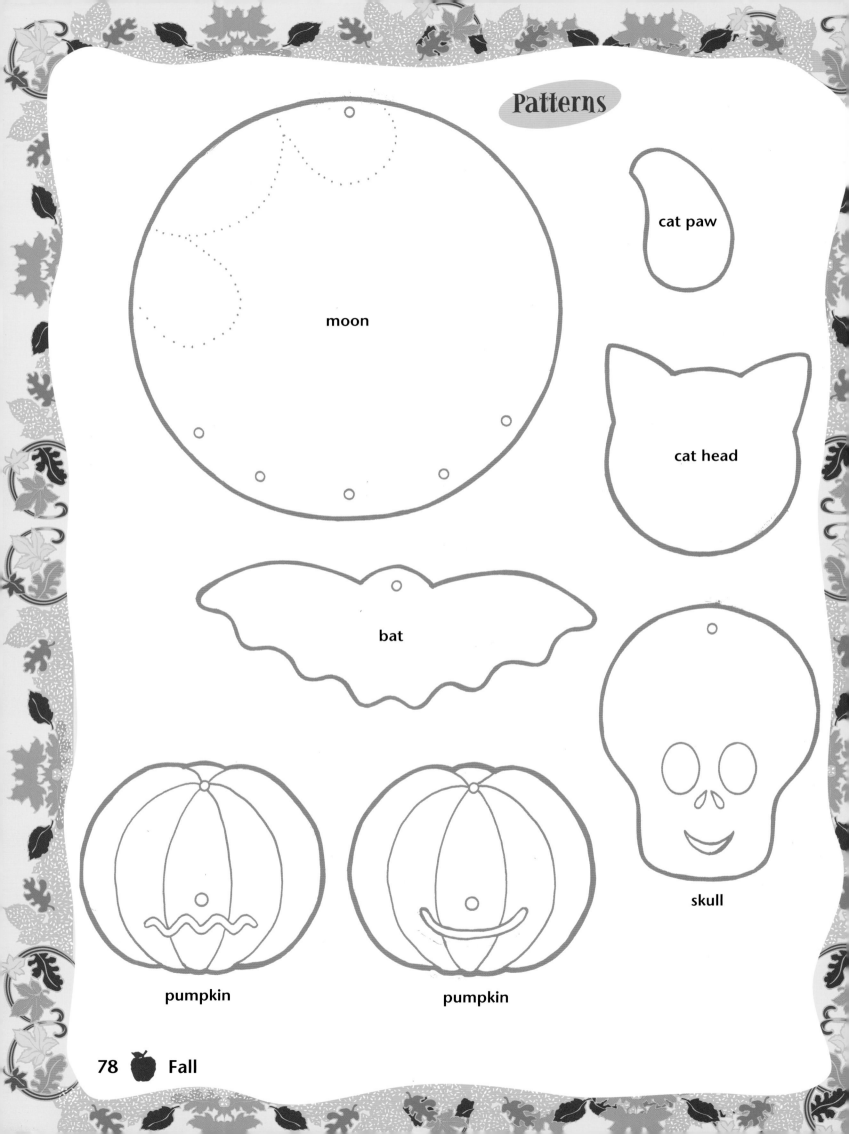

Patterns

moon

cat paw

cat head

bat

skull

pumpkin

pumpkin

Back-to-School Beauties

WHAT YOU'LL NEED

- Ruler
- Pencil
- Foam core
- Craft knife
- Craft glue
- Scrapbook paper
- Matching ribbon
- Scissors
- Velcro hook and loop fasteners

Adult help needed

Bulletin Board

1 Measure the width of the inside of your locker door, and subtract 1 inch to determine the width of the bulletin board. The height for the board is 11 inches. Lay the foam core flat, then ask an adult to help you mark and cut out 2 pieces of foam core with the craft knife according to your measurements. Glue the pieces together with the craft glue.

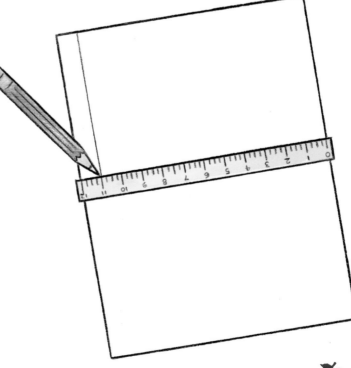

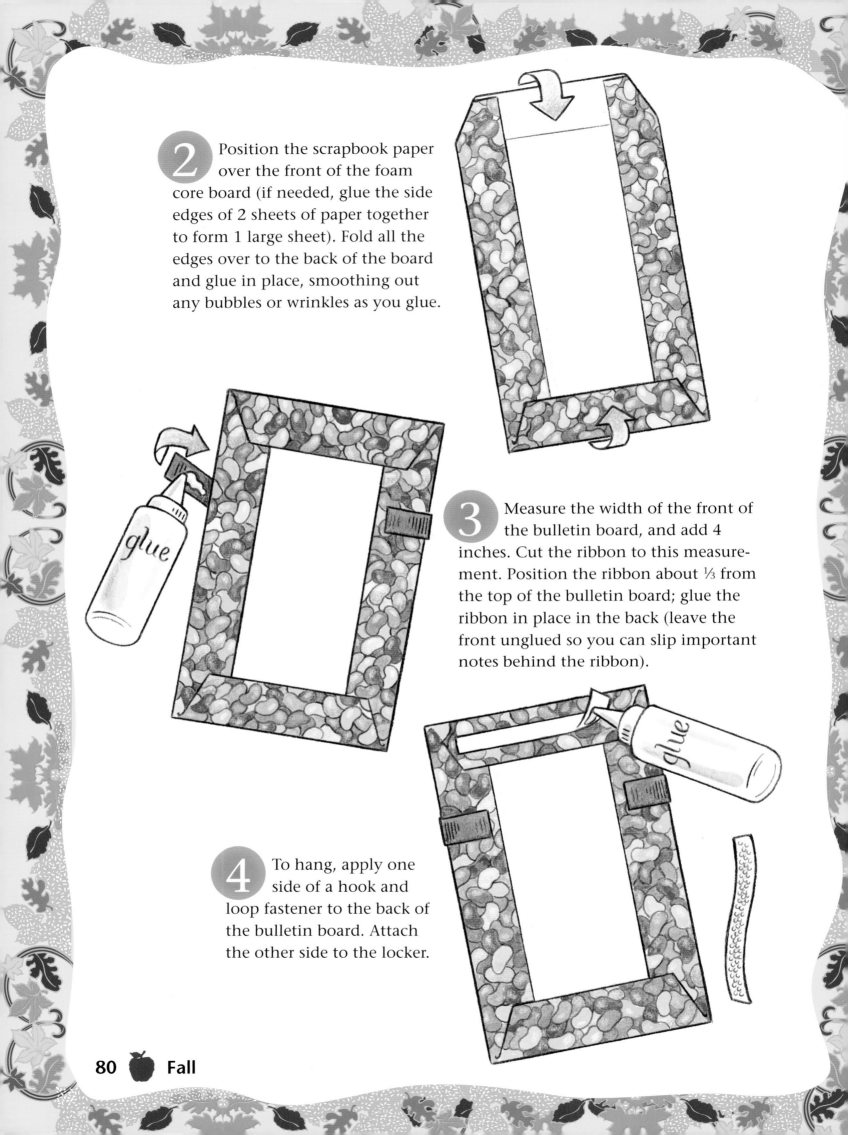

2 Position the scrapbook paper over the front of the foam core board (if needed, glue the side edges of 2 sheets of paper together to form 1 large sheet). Fold all the edges over to the back of the board and glue in place, smoothing out any bubbles or wrinkles as you glue.

3 Measure the width of the front of the bulletin board, and add 4 inches. Cut the ribbon to this measurement. Position the ribbon about ⅓ from the top of the bulletin board; glue the ribbon in place in the back (leave the front unglued so you can slip important notes behind the ribbon).

4 To hang, apply one side of a hook and loop fastener to the back of the bulletin board. Attach the other side to the locker.

Notebook Cover

1 Position the scrapbook paper over the front of a notebook (if needed, glue the side edges of 2 sheets of paper together to form 1 large sheet). Cut a notch at the top and bottom of the paper where the notebook's spine falls. Then turn all the edges to the inside of the notebook and glue in place, smoothing out any bubbles and wrinkles.

2 Measure the width of the front and back of the notebook, then add 16 inches. Cut the ribbon to this measurement. Position the ribbon around the center front and back of the notebook, and glue in place. When dry, tie the ribbons together.

Try This!

You can make Back-to-School Beauties out of lots of things—textbooks, mini notepads, you name it! Just follow the basic techniques listed for the bulletin board and notebook cover.

Spooky Tic-Tac-Toe

WHAT YOU'LL NEED

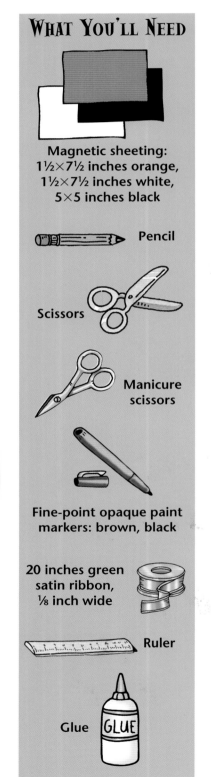

Magnetic sheeting:
1½×7½ inches orange,
1½×7½ inches white,
5×5 inches black

Pencil

Scissors

Manicure scissors

Fine-point opaque paint markers: brown, black

20 inches green satin ribbon, ⅛ inch wide

Ruler

Glue

1 Use the stencils in the back of this book to trace and cut out 5 pumpkins from the orange magnetic sheeting and 5 ghosts from the white magnetic sheeting. When cutting the magnetic sheeting, you may need to use manicure scissors for small curves.

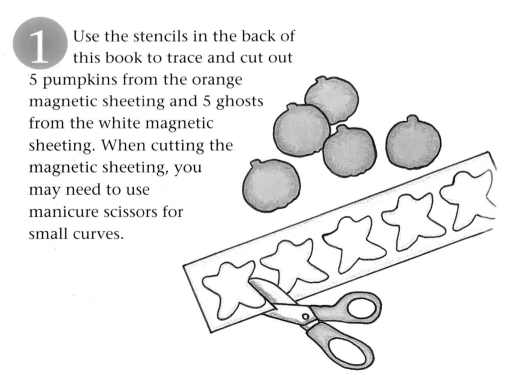

2 Draw a stem and lines on the pumpkins with the brown marker; let dry. Draw faces on the pumpkins with the black marker. Let dry.

3 Draw eyes and mouths on the ghosts with black marker; let dry.

4 Cut the ribbon into four 5-inch lengths. Glue the 4 lengths of ribbon to the black magnetic sheeting to make a tic-tac-toe grid. Now you're ready to play a spooky game of tic-tac-toe!

Harvest Bookmark

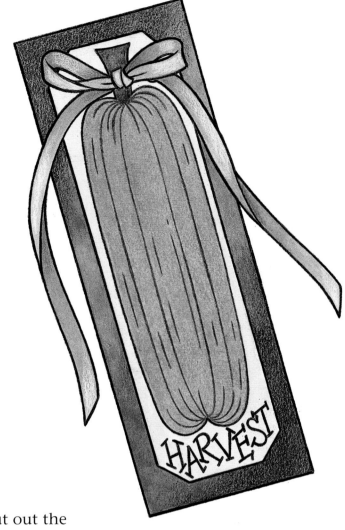

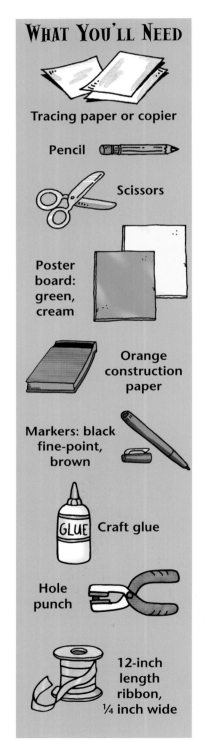
1 Trace and cut out the bookmark frame pattern on page 85 from the green poster board. Repeat for the bookmark insert pattern from the cream poster board and the pumpkin from the orange construction paper. If possible, use a copier to transfer the pumpkin pattern to orange construction paper so the detail lines will be visible. Otherwise, add the detail lines on the pumpkin with the black permanent marker. Color in the stem with the brown marker.

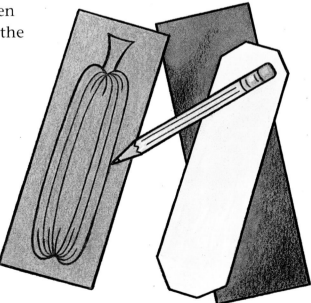

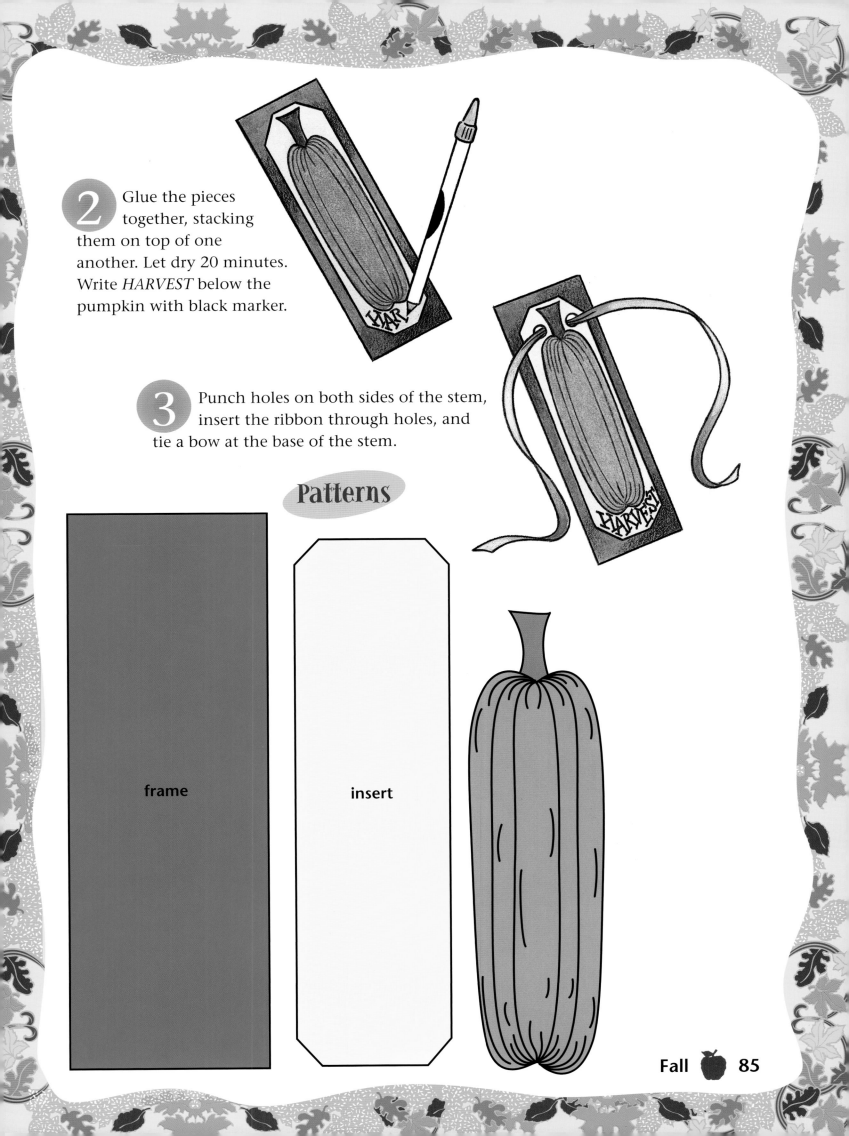

2 Glue the pieces together, stacking them on top of one another. Let dry 20 minutes. Write *HARVEST* below the pumpkin with black marker.

3 Punch holes on both sides of the stem, insert the ribbon through holes, and tie a bow at the base of the stem.

Patterns

frame

insert

Bat-Wing Bracelet

WHAT YOU'LL NEED

- Black construction paper
- Pencil
- Scissors
- Puffy paints
- Glitter
- Glue
- Stapler and staples
- Rubber band

1 Trace and cut out 2 or 3 bat patterns from the stencil in the back of this book onto the black construction paper. Decorate the bats with puffy paints and glitter.

2 When the bats are completely dry, stack 2 or 3 bats on top of each other. Staple the bats together in the center.

3 Place a rubber band over the back of the staple, and staple the rubber band to the bats. Fan out the bat wings, and wear around your wrist as a spooky accessory!

Christmas Window Decorations

What You'll Need

Tracing paper

Pencil

5 pieces cardboard, 6×6 inches each

Masking tape

Plastic wrap

Dimensional paint: red, white, green, glittering gold

Paper towels

Straight pin

Scissors

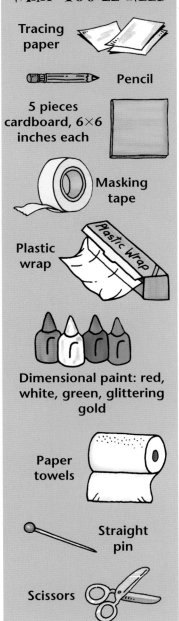

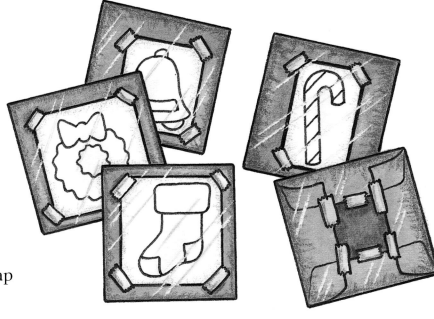

1 Trace the patterns on page 89 onto individual pieces of paper, then tape each piece of paper to a piece of cardboard. Tightly cover each pattern with plastic wrap, and tape the edges of the plastic wrap to the back of the cardboard.

2 Carefully paint the plastic wrap using the pattern as a guide (refer to the illustration for color direction). Work with 1 color at a time, and let each color set for 10 minutes before you paint with the next color. Follow these tips for using dimensional paint: Outline the part of the pattern you're going to paint; lightly touch the tip of the bottle to the plastic wrap, carefully squeeze the bottle, and pull (don't push) the tip along the outline (the paint should be about ⅛ inch thick). Then paint inside the outlined area, working from left to right (or right to left if you're left-handed) and top to bottom. If you make a mistake, wipe the paint off with a paper towel. If the tip of the bottle clogs, use a straight pin to open the hole and then squeeze a bit of paint on a paper scrap to regain a smooth flow.

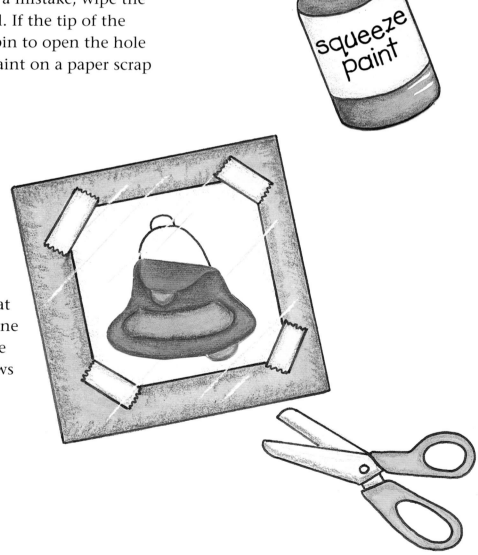

3 Let the paint dry for 24 hours. Peel the decorations off the plastic wrap. Trim off any paint that has spread beyond the outline of the decorations. Hang the decorations on your windows for happy holiday cheer!

Patterns

Heartbreaker

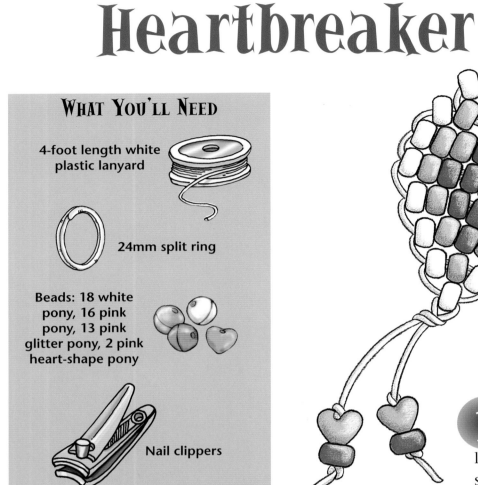

1 Make a lark's head knot by folding the lanyard in half and slipping the looped end through the split ring. Pull the cut ends up through the loop and pull tight. Tie an overhand knot about ½ to 1 inch from the lark's head knot.

2 String a white bead onto the left strand and slide it all the way up to the knot. Weave the right strand through the bead from right to left. To make the heart's upper arches, weave a "sidepath" by stringing beads 1–4 on the right strand. Leave a little space between the beads, and weave back through beads 1 and 2. Pull tightly as you weave back, allowing the beads to curve as shown. Repeat to make a sidepath with the left strand. Add a white bead on the end of each sidepath before you move on to the next row.

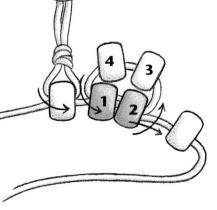

3 String beads onto the left strand in the following order: 1 white, 2 pink, 1 pink glitter, 1 pink, 1 pink glitter, 2 pink, and 1 white. Weave the right strand through the same beads from right to left. Repeat this basic bead-weaving technique for the remaining rows, using the bead diagram for reference.

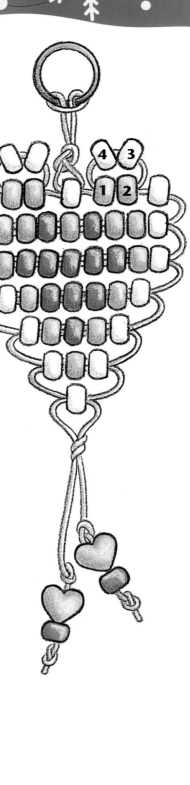

4 Finish by tying both cord ends together in an overhand knot. To do this, twist both lanyard ends into a loop and then pull the free ends through the loop. Tie a second overhand knot on each cord about 1½ to 2 inches from the first knot. String a heart pony bead and a glitter bead on each cord, and finish each with another overhand knot. Trim the excess cord with the nail clippers, leaving ½-inch tails.

Sensational Spiral Ornament

WHAT YOU'LL NEED

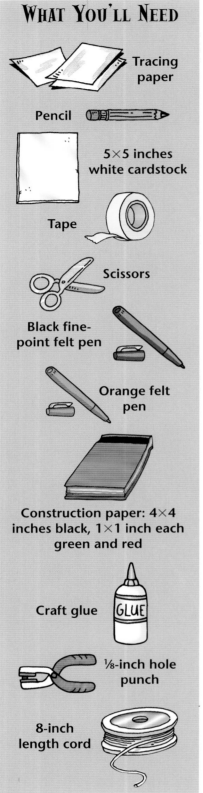

Tracing paper

Pencil

5×5 inches white cardstock

Tape

Scissors

Black fine-point felt pen

Orange felt pen

Construction paper: 4×4 inches black, 1×1 inch each green and red

Craft glue

⅛-inch hole punch

8-inch length cord

1 Trace or photocopy the patterns on page 93. Tape the spiral pattern to the cardstock, and cut along the lines of the pattern. Remove the pattern.

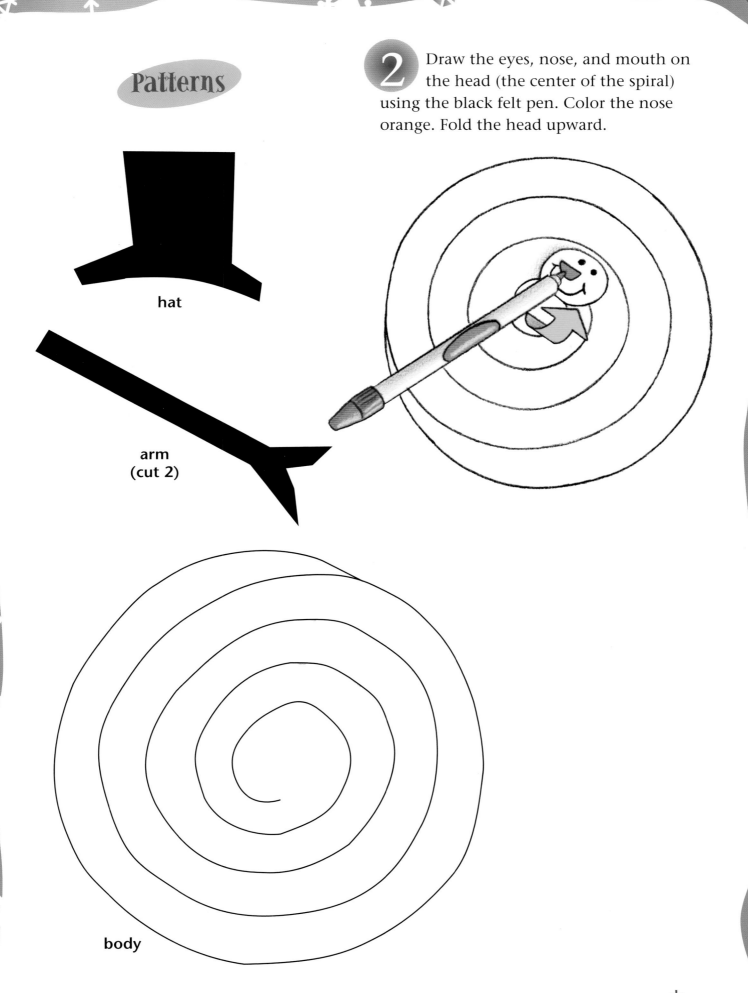

Patterns

hat

arm
(cut 2)

body

2 Draw the eyes, nose, and mouth on the head (the center of the spiral) using the black felt pen. Color the nose orange. Fold the head upward.

3 Cut out the patterns for the arm and the hat. Trace around the arm pattern twice on the black paper and cut out. Fold the remaining piece of black paper in half, and place the top edge of the hat pattern along the fold. Trace around the pattern, and cut it out (don't cut the fold). Apply glue to the inside of the hat, and slip it over the snowman's head. Press the hat pieces together, sandwiching the top of the head between. Glue an arm to each side of the first spiral below the head.

4 From the green paper, cut out 2 holly leaves. Use the hole punch to make a red berry from the red paper. Glue the holly leaves and the berry to the hat.

5 Punch a hole in the top of the hat. Fold the cord in half and tie the ends of the cord together. Push the cord loop through the hole, and thread the tied ends of the cord through the loop of the cord. Hang your spiral friend on a Christmas tree or wherever you like!

Hanukkah Banner

Adult help needed

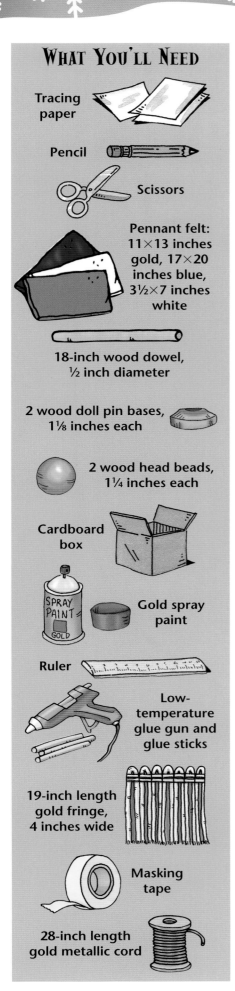

What You'll Need

Tracing paper

Pencil

Scissors

Pennant felt: 11×13 inches gold, 17×20 inches blue, 3½×7 inches white

18-inch wood dowel, ½ inch diameter

2 wood doll pin bases, 1⅛ inches each

2 wood head beads, 1¼ inches each

Cardboard box

Gold spray paint

Ruler

Low-temperature glue gun and glue sticks

19-inch length gold fringe, 4 inches wide

Masking tape

28-inch length gold metallic cord

1 Using the pattern on page 96, trace and cut out the menorah from the gold felt. Working with an adult in a well-ventilated area, place the menorah, the dowel, the 2 doll pin bases, and the 2 head beads in the cardboard box. Spray all with 2 coats of gold spray paint. Let dry.

Patterns

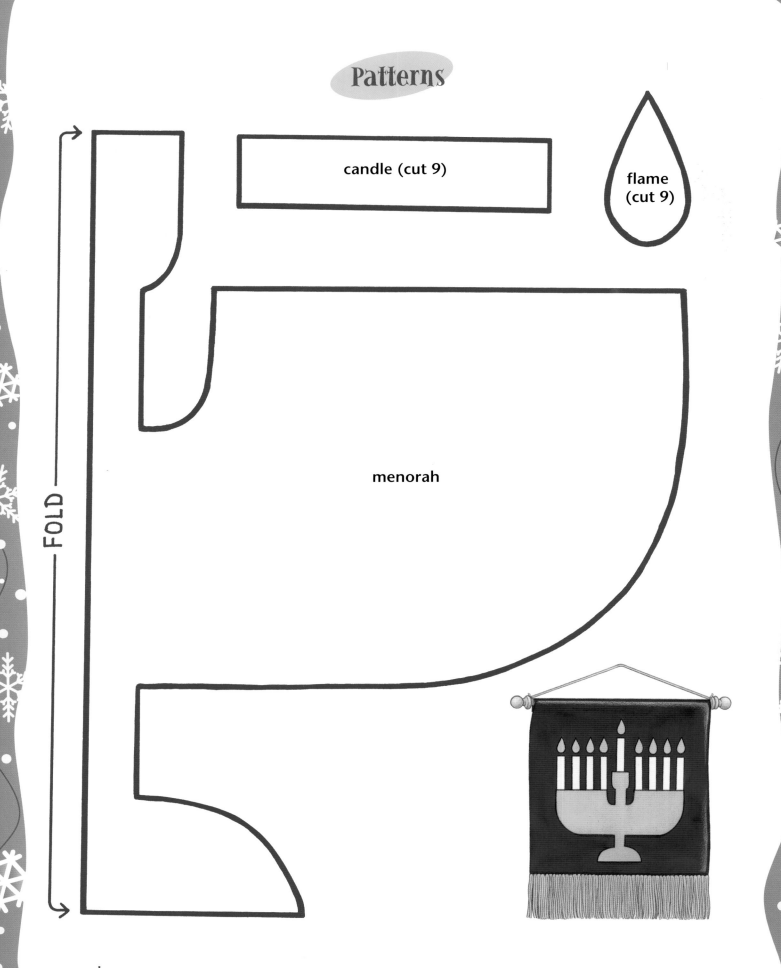

candle (cut 9)

flame (cut 9)

FOLD

menorah

2 To make a hem in the 17-inch side of the blue felt, fold over 2 inches of the felt and crease it. Unfold, then apply a line of glue ¼ inch from the edge and refold the felt. Hold it in place until the glue dries. Be sure to leave enough room between the crease and the glue line to insert the dowel.

4 Glue the fringe to the bottom of the banner so 1 inch of fringe sticks out from each side. Fold and glue the 1-inch sections of fringe to the back of the banner. Position the menorah and candles as shown in the illustration, then glue them to the banner. Roll 9 pieces of masking tape into loops with the sticky side out, and put one on the back of each flame. (You can add 1 flame to the banner on each day of Hanukkah.)

3 Using the patterns on page 96, trace and cut out 9 candles from the white pennant felt and 9 flames from the gold felt.

5 Slide the dowel through the hem at the top of the banner. Glue a head bead to a doll pin base, then glue them to one end of the dowel. Repeat on the other end of the dowel. To make a hanger, tie the ends of the cord to the ends of the dowel.

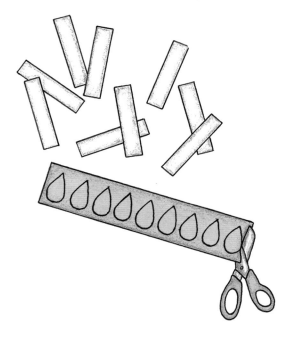

Tracing paper

Pencil

Scissors

2 sheets opaque shrink plastic, 8¼×10¾ inches each

Sandpaper

Black medium-point permanent marker

Acrylic paint: pink, light brown

Paintbrushes

Hole punch

Cookie sheet

Aluminum foil

34 inches white baby rickrack

Ruler

Craft glue

4 wiggle eyes, 7mm each

Tweezers

1×1 inches green felt

3 red buttons, ⅛ inch each

2-inch length green eyelet lace, 1 inch wide

6-inch length red satin ribbon, ⅛ inch wide

16 inches red rattail cord

Gingerbread Kid Ornaments

1 Trace and cut out gingerbread pattern on page 99. Lightly sand both sheets of shrink plastic, then trace pattern on each sheet with the marker. Paint pink circles for the cheeks, then paint the rest of the shape with a thin coat of light brown; let dry. Cut out each shape. Punch a hole in each, ½ inch down from the top of the head. Place the cutouts on a foil-covered cookie sheet, then follow the manufacturer's instructions for baking. Let cool.

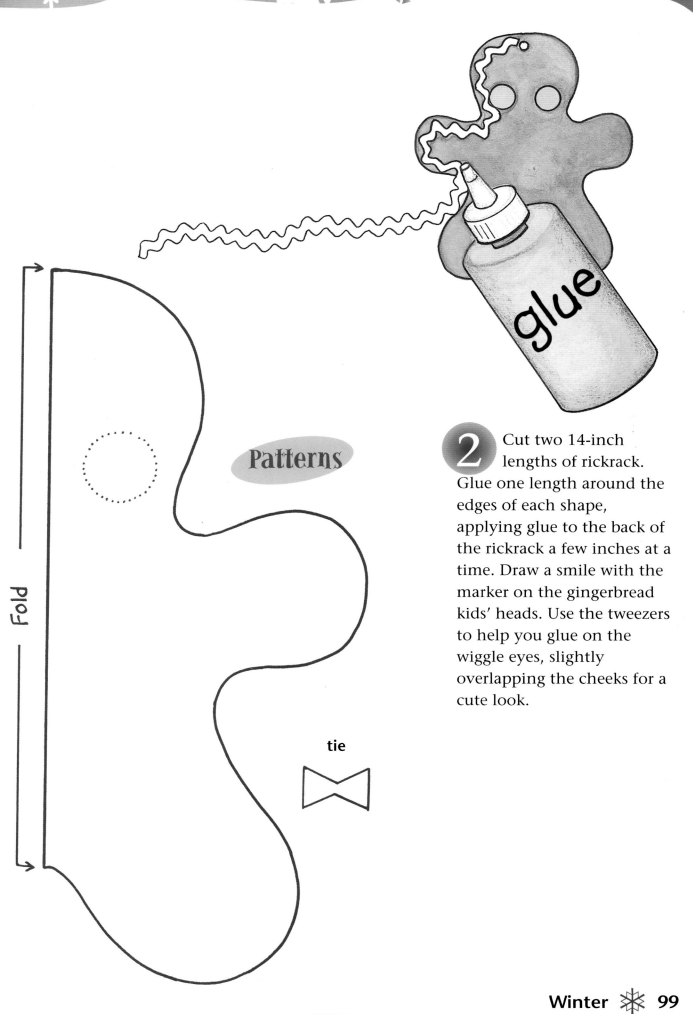

Patterns

Fold

tie

glue

2 Cut two 14-inch lengths of rickrack. Glue one length around the edges of each shape, applying glue to the back of the rickrack a few inches at a time. Draw a smile with the marker on the gingerbread kids' heads. Use the tweezers to help you glue on the wiggle eyes, slightly overlapping the cheeks for a cute look.

3 Using the pattern on page 99, trace and cut out the tie from the green felt. Glue the tie to the neck of one of the ornaments. Finish this ornament by gluing 3 red buttons down the front.

4 For the second ornament, begin by gluing lace across the waist. Tie the ribbon into a bow, and glue it to the neck. For hair, glue the center of two 3-inch lengths of rickrack to the top of the head. Spot-glue hair at the sides of the head.

5 For the hanger loops, cut two 8-inch lengths of rattail cord. Insert the end of one length through the hole in the ornament and tie the ends together in a knot. Repeat for the other ornament.

My Kwanza Family

WHAT YOU'LL NEED

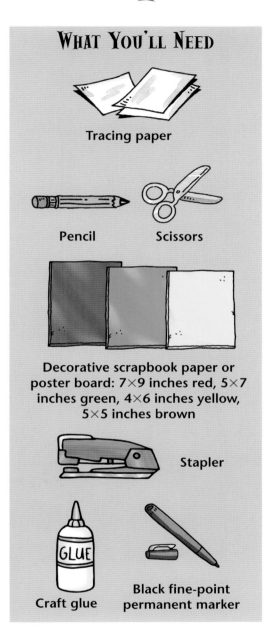

Tracing paper

Pencil   Scissors

Decorative scrapbook paper or poster board: 7×9 inches red, 5×7 inches green, 4×6 inches yellow, 5×5 inches brown

Stapler

GLUE

Craft glue   Black fine-point permanent marker

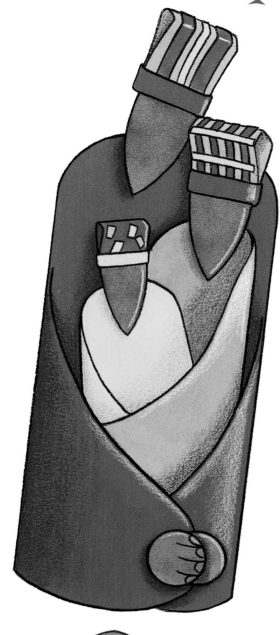

1. Trace and cut out the father's body pattern from page 102 on red poster board or scrapbook paper. Repeat for the mother's body pattern using green paper and the child's body pattern using yellow paper. Trace and cut out 2 head patterns for the mother and father, 1 child's head, and 2 father's hands from brown paper. Trace and cut out 2 hat patterns for the mother and father using green paper and 1 child's hat pattern from red paper. Set aside.

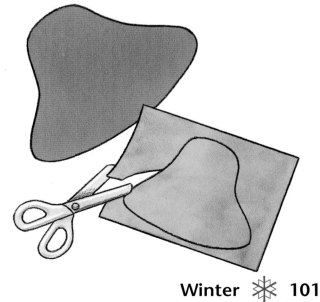

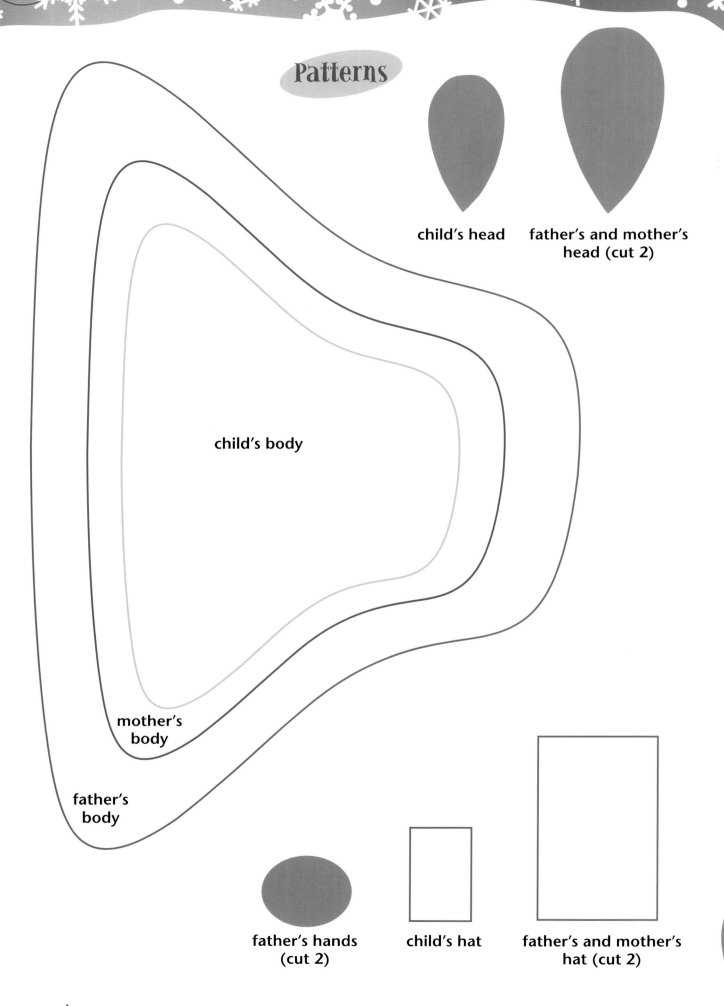

Patterns

child's head

father's and mother's head (cut 2)

child's body

mother's body

father's body

father's hands (cut 2)

child's hat

father's and mother's hat (cut 2)

2 Bring the "arm" parts of the father's "body" together, overlapping the arms in front and stapling them together. Repeat with mother and child cutouts. Glue heads onto the bodies of the mother, father, and child.

4 Insert the bodies one inside the other, turning them so the child is cradled at the center of the family. Draw the fingers on the father's hands with the black marker, then glue them to the front.

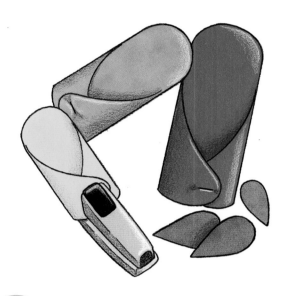

3 Decorate the hats with leftover paper or poster board scraps. Let dry. Fold the father's hat in half, bringing the short ends together, and staple or glue the hat to the father's head. Glue a strip of paper around the bottom of the hat to cover the staple and act like a hatband. Repeat for the mother's hat and the child's hat.

Did You Know?

Kwanza means "the first" or "the first fruits of the harvest" in Kiswahili. (Kiswahili is an East African language.) Dr. Maulana Karenga began the holiday in 1966 to celebrate the rich cultural roots of African-American people.

Super Snowman Magnet

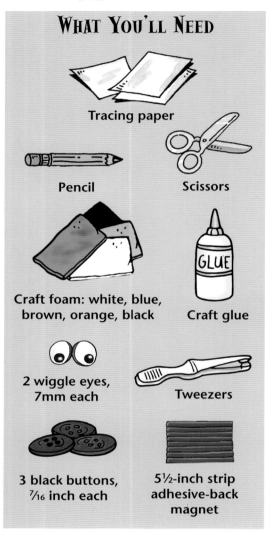

1 Trace and cut out the patterns on page 105.

2 Using the patterns, trace the shapes on the following colors of foam: snowman body on white, scarf on blue, twig arms on brown (make 2), carrot nose on orange, and hat on black. Cut out the pieces.

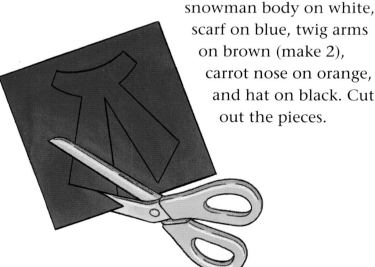

Patterns

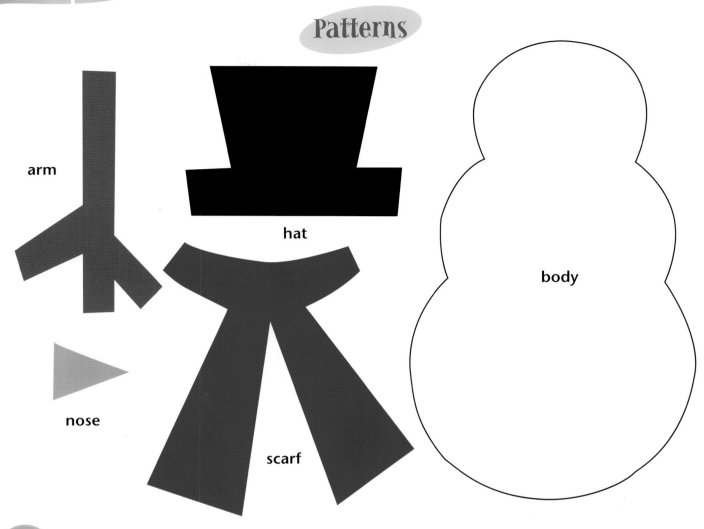

arm

hat

body

nose

scarf

3 With the craft glue, attach the hat to the snowman's head, the scarf around the neck, the twig arms on both sides of the snowman's upper body, and the nose to the middle of the face. Use tweezers to help you glue the wiggle eyes above the nose. Glue the buttons down the center of the body.

4 Peel the backing off the magnet strip, and attach the magnet to the back of the snowman.

Christmas Tree Shirt

Adult help needed

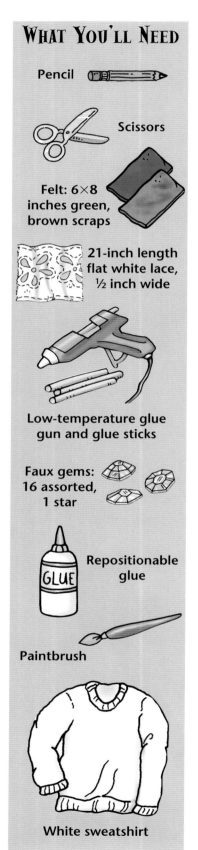
1 Using the stencil in the back of the book, trace and cut out the tree from the green felt. Cut a small tree trunk out of the brown felt.

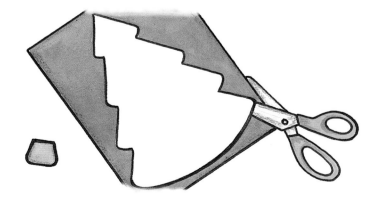

2 For the tree garland, use the glue gun to attach one end of the lace to the top left of the tree. Drape the lace back and forth across the tree, folding over and gluing the lace each time it changes direction. When needed, add a spot of glue to any curves to keep the lace flat against the felt. Use the glue gun to randomly attach the gems to the tree. Glue the star gem at the top. Glue the edge of the trunk under the bottom center of the tree so the tree overlaps the trunk about ½ inch.

3 Turn the tree over and apply 2 or 3 coats of the repositionable glue according to the manufacturer's instructions. Let the glue dry for 24 hours, then attach the tree to the front of the sweatshirt. Remove the tree before washing.

Try This!

Don't want a Christmas tree shirt? No problem! Just make a different shape out of felt and follow the instructions above to attach it to your sweatshirt.

Happy Hanukkah Paper

WHAT YOU'LL NEED

Pencil

Compressed sponge

Scissors

Paper towels

Kraft paper

Acrylic paint: blue, yellow, white

3 foam plates

Old toothbrush

1 Use the stencils in the back of the book to help you trace and cut out a dreidel and Star of David shape from the compressed sponge. Run the sponge shapes under water, and press out any excess water with paper towels.

2 Cut the kraft paper to the size you need to wrap a gift. Pour blue and yellow paint onto foam plates. Dip the Star of David sponge into yellow paint, coating one side. Sponge the star over the kraft paper, pressing the sponge onto the paper. (You will probably have to dip the sponge into the paint a few times to cover the paper with stars.) Let dry.

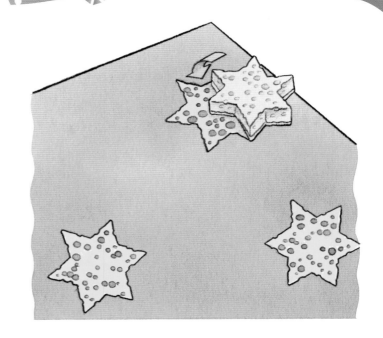

3 Now use the dreidel sponge and blue paint to add dreidels to your gift wrap. Let dry.

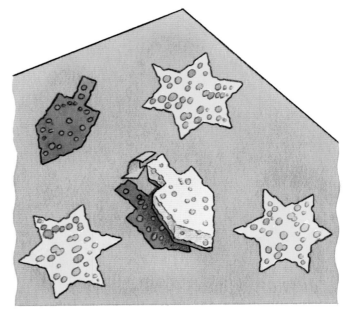

4 Pour the white paint onto a foam plate, then load an old toothbrush with the paint. To spatter-paint the paper, hold the brush over the paper, and run your finger over the bristles. Let dry. Wrap a Hanukkah gift with the paper, and add a matching ribbon for that extra-special touch!

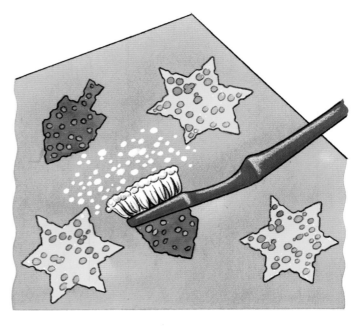

International Christmas Ornaments

Adult help needed

What You'll Need

Tracing paper

Pencil

Scissors

Green poster board

Craft knife

Red plastic tape, ¾ inch wide

Ruler

Hole punch

Craft glue

Glitter

8½×11-inch sheet white paper

Red construction paper

Shiny red and white gift wrap

Paper Cornucopia

1 Using the pattern on page 111, trace and cut out the triangle shape. Trace the triangle onto the green poster board 4 times, repositioning it as shown. Cut out the shape along the outer lines only.

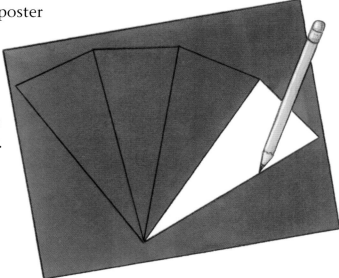

Pattern

2 Ask an adult to help you score the 3 interior lines with the craft knife. Bend the poster board along the scored lines.

3 Cut three 6½-inch pieces of plastic tape. Have an adult help you use the ruler and craft knife to cut the pieces in half lengthwise (making six ⅜-inch-wide strips). Tape the 2 cut edges of the poster board together, taking care to center the tape along the edge. Trim the excess tape at the bottom and top edges of the cone. Tape the other 3 edges of the cone. Use the remaining strips to tape around the edge of the cone.

4 Punch a hole in opposite sides of the cone. Fold a 12-inch length of plastic tape lengthwise, sticky sides together, to make a hanging ribbon. Insert one end of the ribbon in each of the holes and tie an overhand knot on each end inside the cone. Make a long squiggle of craft glue on one side of the cone. Sprinkle glitter on the glue, then gently knock off the excess glitter. Let dry completely.

Pleated Fan

1 Fold the white paper in half along its length. Cut along the crease line to make two 8½×5½-inch rectangles. Pleat the paper by accordion-folding it, back and forth, in ¼-inch folds. Cut off the last fold with scissors if it is less than the full width.

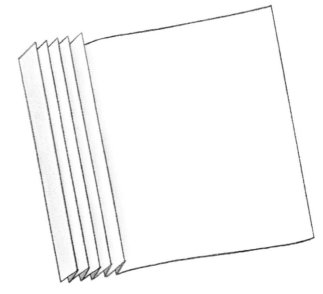

2 Bunching the folds together, cut one end of the pleated paper at an angle. Make a series of small triangular cuts halfway along both sides of the pleats.

3 Cut two ¼-inch-wide strips from the red construction paper, one 3 inches long, the other 6 inches long. Glue the ends of the longer strip to each side of the uncut end of the pleated paper to make a hanging loop. Glue the shorter strip around the base of the loop; trim any excess. Spread out the pleats.

Scandinavian Heart Basket

1 Measure and cut a 3×9-inch rectangle out of both the red and the white gift wrap. Fold the red rectangle in half so the short ends meet. At the folded edge, measure and cut 2 lines 1 inch apart and 3⅛ inches long. Round the opposite corners. Repeat for the white rectangle.

2 Open up the top red strip and insert the top white strip between the layers. Then insert the red strip between the layers of the middle white strip. Insert the bottom white strip between the layers of the red strip. The middle red strip is woven between the top white, over the middle white, and between the bottom white strips. The bottom red strip is woven the same as the top red strip.

3 Cut a ½-inch-wide handle from the red gift wrap. Fold it in half, and glue the ends to the inside of the basket.

Valentine Candy Magnet

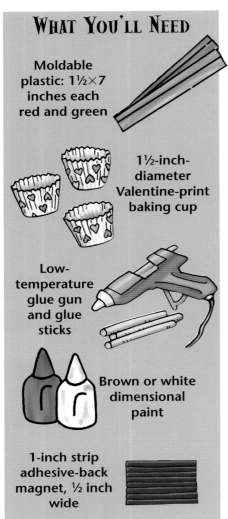

What You'll Need

Moldable plastic: 1½×7 inches each red and green

1½-inch-diameter Valentine-print baking cup

Low-temperature glue gun and glue sticks

Brown or white dimensional paint

1-inch strip adhesive-back magnet, ½ inch wide

1 Place the strips of moldable plastic in warm water until they are soft. Knead and mix the 2 strips together until they are a uniform brown color. You may have to resoften the plastic a couple of times to remove all the streaks of red and green. Roll the plastic between your palms to form a smooth ball. Flatten one side of the ball slightly by gently pushing it down onto your work surface. Allow the plastic ball to set.

2 Glue the flattened side of the ball to the bottom of the baking cup. Glue the sides of the baking cup to the sides of the ball in 3 or 4 places. Paint wavy lines across the top of the ball with the dimensional paint. Let dry.

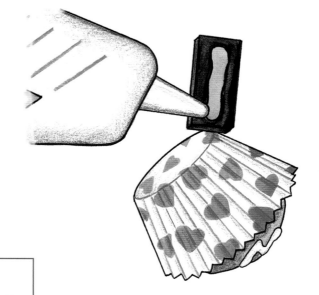

3 Attach the magnet strip to the bottom or back side of the baking cup. Repeat all the steps to fill your refrigerator with delicious-looking "candy" magnets!

Did You Know?

The original St. Valentine lived during the time of Roman Emperor Claudius II, who wanted the men in the army to stay unmarried. But St. Valentine would secretly marry the men and their sweethearts.

Candy Cane Doorknob Decoration

What You'll Need

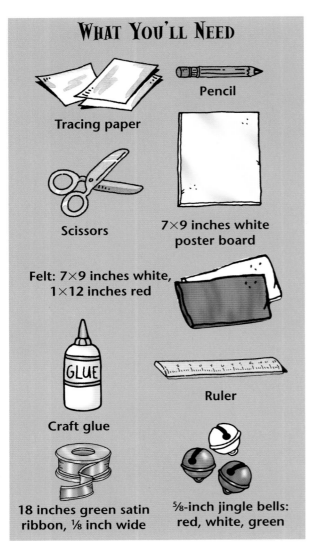

Tracing paper

Pencil

Scissors

7×9 inches white poster board

Felt: 7×9 inches white, 1×12 inches red

GLUE

Craft glue

Ruler

18 inches green satin ribbon, ⅛ inch wide

⅝-inch jingle bells: red, white, green

1 Using the stencil in the back of the book, trace and cut out 4 candy canes—two from poster board and two from white felt. Lay the poster board canes on your work surface so the top curves face the center. Starting on the left side, glue one felt cane to each poster board cane.

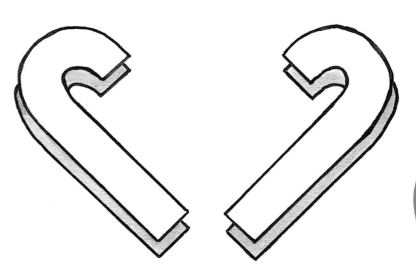

2 To make the stripes, cut the red felt into two ½×12-inch lengths. Then cut each length into four 2-inch lengths and one 4-inch length. Before gluing, place the stripes diagonally on the canes with the 4-inch lengths at the top curves. The ends of the stripes will overlap the edges of the canes. One at a time, glue the stripes onto the canes. Let dry, then turn over each cane. Trim any excess red felt so the ends are even with the edges of the white felt.

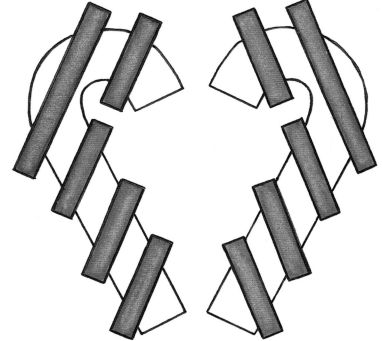

3 To assemble the doorknob decoration, overlap the canes at the top and bottom to form a heart shape. Glue together the overlapping areas. Cut the ribbon so you have 3-, 4-, 5-, and 6-inch lengths. To attach the bells, insert one end of the 3-inch length of ribbon through the red bell loop. Bring the ends of the ribbon together and glue. Repeat using the 4-inch length of ribbon with the white bell and the 5-inch length with the green bell. Glue the ribbon ends to the back bottom of the canes. Tie the 6-inch length of ribbon into a bow, and glue it to the front bottom of the canes.

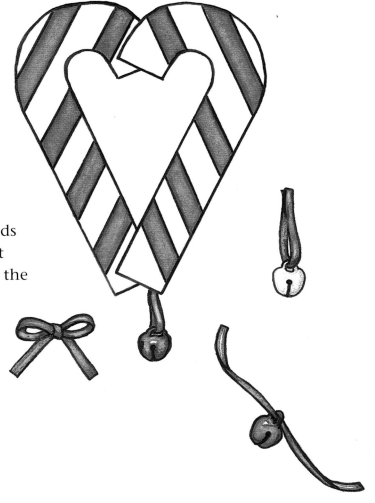

Pom Reindeer Magnet

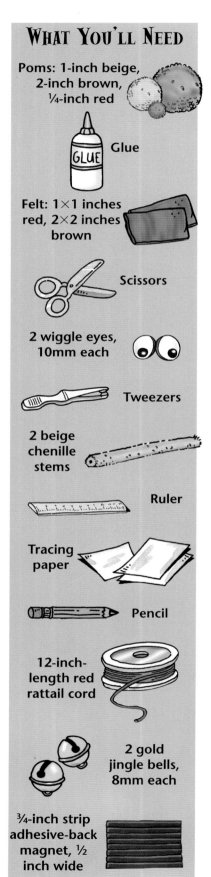

1 To make the reindeer's head and the muzzle, glue the beige pom to the lower front part of the brown pom. For the nose, glue the red pom to the upper front part of the muzzle. Cut a smiling mouth shape from the red felt, and glue it below the nose. Glue the wiggle eyes to the head so the bottom edges of the eyes touch the top of the muzzle (you may want to use tweezers to help you glue on the eyes).

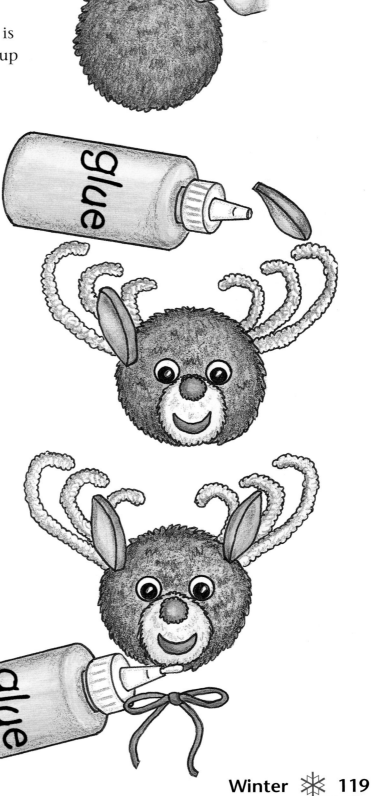

2 Measure and cut 1 chenille stem into a 5-inch length and a 7-inch length. Cut the other chenille stem in half; you will use only one of the 6-inch lengths, so set the other length aside. To make the antlers, line up the middles of the 3 lengths of chenille stem. Twist the stems in the middle to join them together. Arrange the stems so the 7-inch length is on the bottom, the 6-inch length is in between, and the 5-inch length is on top. Pinch and curl each of the six ends up to form the antlers. Glue the middle of the antlers to the back of the head.

3 Using the pattern below, trace and cut 2 ears from the brown felt. Apply a dot of glue to the bottom of 1 ear; pinch the bottom together and hold it for a moment. Repeat this gluing process to make the other ear. Glue the ears to the head just in front of the antlers.

ear
(cut 2)

4 Tie a bow in the rattail cord. Glue the bow beneath the muzzle. Tie a jingle bell to each end of the rattail cord. Attach the magnet strip to the back of the head.

Pinecone Wreath

Adult help needed

WHAT YOU'LL NEED

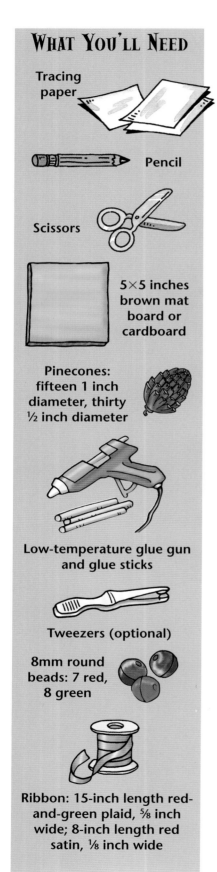

Tracing paper

Pencil

Scissors

5×5 inches brown mat board or cardboard

Pinecones: fifteen 1 inch diameter, thirty ½ inch diameter

Low-temperature glue gun and glue sticks

Tweezers (optional)

8mm round beads: 7 red, 8 green

Ribbon: 15-inch length red-and-green plaid, ⅝ inch wide; 8-inch length red satin, ⅛ inch wide

1 Using the pattern on page 121, trace and cut out a circle from the mat board. Arrange the 1-inch pinecones standing upright in a circle on the mat board so they fit tightly against each other; glue in place.

2 Glue about half of the ½-inch pinecones on their sides on the outer edge of the mat board in the spaces between the 1-inch pinecones. Glue the rest of the ½-inch cones around the inner edge of the mat board in the same way. It might be easier to arrange the pinecones if you use tweezers.

3 Glue the beads onto the wreath as shown in the illustration.

4 Tie a bow in the plaid ribbon, and cut "V" notches in the tail ends. Glue the bow to the top of the wreath. To make a hanger, fold the satin ribbon in half to form a loop, and glue the ends to the back of the mat board at the top of the wreath.

Pattern

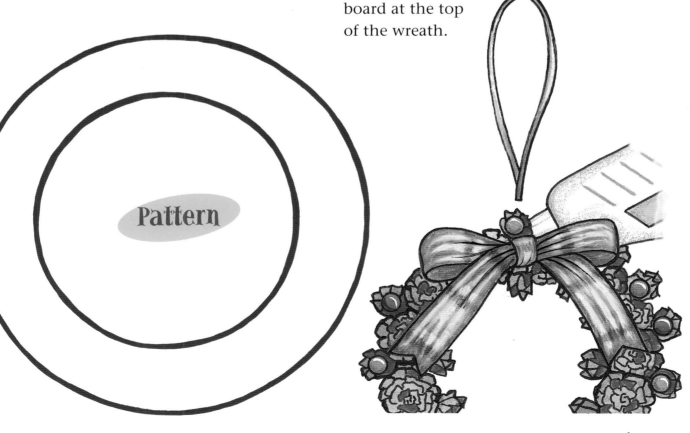

"I Have a Dream" Pencil Holder

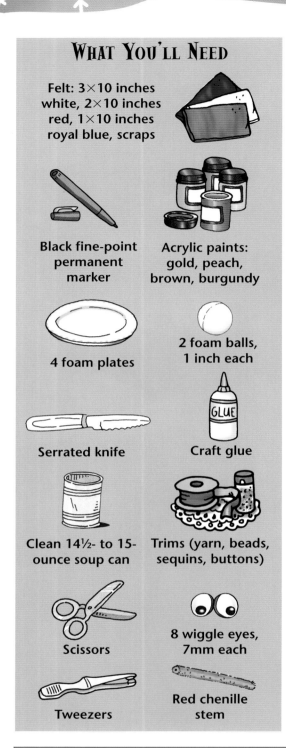
Did You Know?

Dr. Martin Luther King, Jr., delivered his "I Have a Dream" speech at the 1963 March on Washington. His dream was that all people would be treated equally. Today, we honor King's memory with a national holiday on the third Monday in January.

Adult help needed

1 Fold the white felt piece in half, bringing the short ends together. With the permanent marker, draw 2 stick figures. Be sure to leave some space at the top, bottom, and sides of the stick figures for heads, hands, and feet. Unfold the felt, and draw 2 stick figures on the other half.

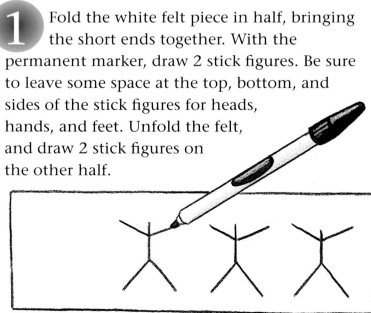

2 Pour a little of each paint color onto separate foam plates. Have an adult help you cut the foam balls in half with the serrated knife to create 4 ball halves. Using a different ball half for each color, dip one at a time into one color of paint, dab off any extra paint, and stamp the ball half onto the felt to make a head on a stick figure. Make the hands and feet by dipping your fingertip into the same color paint and pressing onto the felt. Wipe your finger clean, and move to the next color. Repeat with a different color on all 4 stick figures. Let dry for 24 hours.

3 Glue the long edges of the blue and red felt to the white felt piece. Let dry. Line up the bottom edge of the felt with the bottom of the can and glue the felt to can, wrapping around and overlapping at the ends. Press the top edge of the red felt down into the can and glue in place.

4 "Dress" the stick figures by gluing clothes on them made from felt scraps. For the pants, cut small squares, then cut partway through the middle to make legs. Shirts can be made out of small rectangles; dresses from triangles. Glue on yarn or felt "hair" and decorate clothes and people with felt, glitter, sequins, buttons, and other trim. Use tweezers to help you glue on the wiggle eyes. Glue the red chenille stem around the bottom of the white felt strip, twist the ends to hold, and cut any excess stem.

Kwanza Calendar

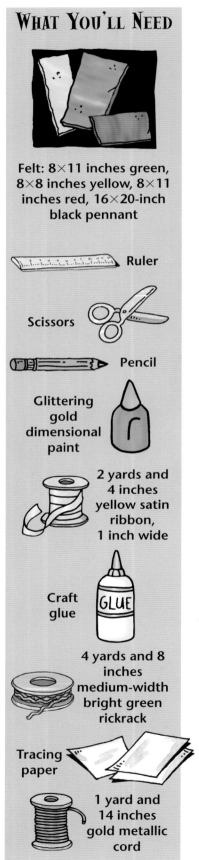

Felt: 8×11 inches green, 8×8 inches yellow, 8×11 inches red, 16×20-inch black pennant

Ruler

Scissors

Pencil

Glittering gold dimensional paint

2 yards and 4 inches yellow satin ribbon, 1 inch wide

Craft glue

4 yards and 8 inches medium-width bright green rickrack

Tracing paper

1 yard and 14 inches gold metallic cord

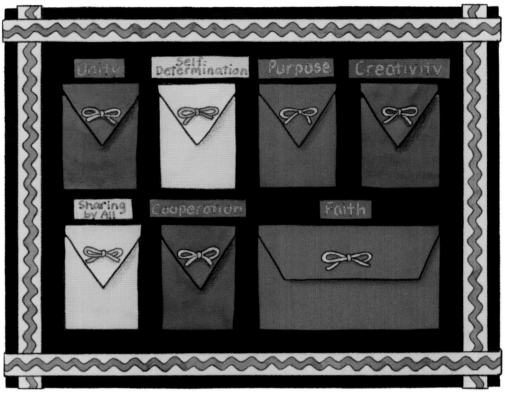

1 Cut 3 green, 2 yellow, and 2 red 1×5-inch pieces of felt. Carefully write the following words on the felt with dimensional paint (you may want to lightly write the words first in pencil): *Unity, Self-Determination, Purpose, Creativity, Sharing by All, Cooperation,* and *Faith.* Let the paint dry, then trim the ends of the felt pieces to within ¼ inch of the words.

2 Cut the ribbon into two 17-inch lengths and two 21-inch lengths. Glue the 17-inch lengths of ribbon vertically on the black felt, ½ inch from the sides. Cut two 17-inch lengths of rickrack, and glue them side by side on top of each 17-inch length of ribbon. Fold over and glue the ends of the 17-inch pieces of ribbon and rickrack to the back of the black felt. Glue two 21-inch lengths of ribbon horizontally on the black felt, ½ inch from the top and bottom. Glue two 21-inch lengths of rickrack side by side on top of each 21-inch length of ribbon. Fold and glue the ends of the 21-inch pieces of ribbon and rickrack over to the back of the black felt.

3 Using the patterns on page 126, trace and cut out pockets and flaps from the felt as follows: 3 small each from green, 2 small each from yellow, 1 small and 1 large each from red.

4 Arrange the pockets, flaps, and words on the black felt as shown. To glue the pockets to the black felt, glue the bottom of each pocket first, then slightly push in the sides of the pocket and glue them. (This will loosen the pockets to allow space for gifts.) Glue the top edge of the flaps about ¼ inch above the pockets. Glue the words above the flaps.

5 Cut seven 6-inch lengths of gold cord. Tie a bow in each length, then evenly trim the ends. Glue a bow to each pocket flap. Turn the calendar over. For hanger loops, cut two 4-inch lengths of gold cord. Fold each length in half to form a loop, and glue the ends of a loop in each of the top corners on the back of the calendar.

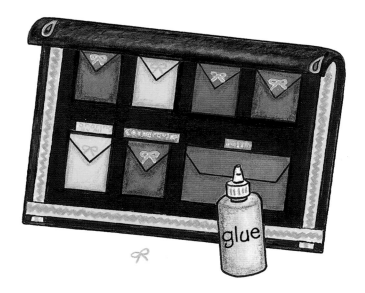

Patterns

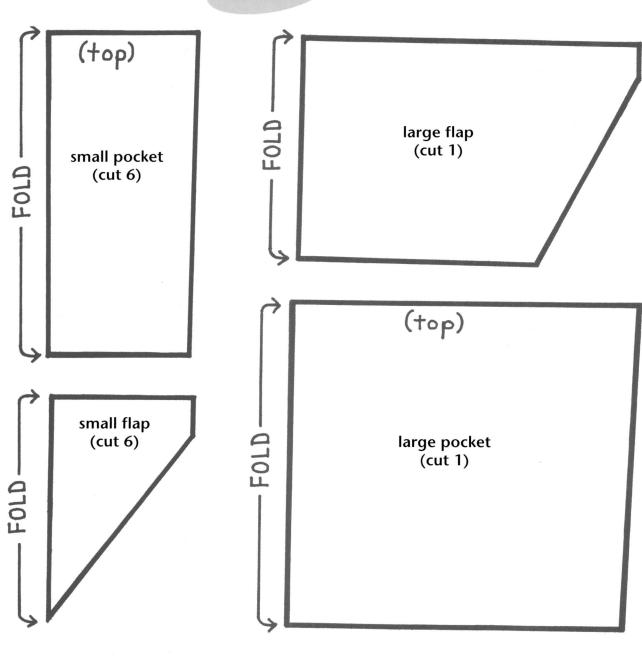

(top)

FOLD

small pocket
(cut 6)

FOLD

large flap
(cut 1)

FOLD

small flap
(cut 6)

(top)

FOLD

large pocket
(cut 1)

Snow Buddy Pencil Topper

What You'll Need

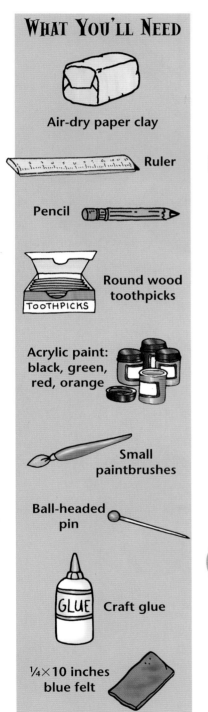

Air-dry paper clay

Ruler

Pencil

Round wood toothpicks

TOOTHPICKS

Acrylic paint: black, green, red, orange

Small paintbrushes

Ball-headed pin

GLUE Craft glue

¼×10 inches blue felt

1 To make the body of the snow buddy, roll a 1-inch ball of clay. Insert the end of the pencil halfway into the body. Break a wood toothpick in half, and insert half of it into the center top of the body.

2 Make the head by rolling a ⅞-inch ball of clay. Insert this into the toothpick on top of the snow buddy's body. Slightly flatten the top of the head.

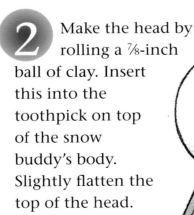

3 To make the hat, flatten a ⅝-inch ball of clay into a 1⅛-inch circle. Roll a ⅞-inch ball, and slightly flatten the top and bottom of it (the sides should stay rounded). Place the flattened ball on the brim to complete the hat.

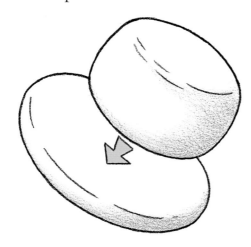

4 Flatten a 2-inch ball of clay, and cut out 2 holly leaves with a toothpick. Make lines in the center of the leaves with the end of the toothpick. Roll a small ball of clay, then roll a ⅛-inch ball into a carrot shape. Let the body, hat, leaves, small ball, and carrot shape dry for 24 hours.

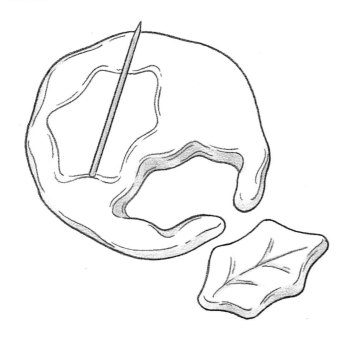

5 When the pieces have dried, paint the hat black, the holly leaves green, the small ball red, and the carrot nose orange. Use the ball-head of the pin and the black paint to dot eyes and a mouth on the snow buddy's face. Let the paint dry completely.

6 Glue the holly leaves and the red ball to the top of the hat. Glue the hat to the top of the snow buddy's head and the carrot nose to the snow buddy's face. Tie the piece of blue felt around the snow buddy's neck, and glue the ends down.